Workbook 9

Budgeting and Financial Control

Manage Res[illegible]
Certifica[illegible]
S/NVQ Le[illegible]

Institute of Management Open Learning Programme

Series editor: Gareth Lewis
Author: Cathy Lake

chartered
management
institute

Pergamon
Flexible
Learning

OXFORD AMSTERDAM BOSTON LONDON NEW YORK PARIS
SAN DIEGO SAN FRANCISCO SINGAPORE SYDNEY TOKYO

Pergamon Flexible Learning
An imprint of Elsevier Science
Linacre House, Jordan Hill, Oxford OX2 8DP
225 Wildwood Avenue, Woburn, MA 01801-2041

First published 1997
Reprinted 1999, 2000, 2001, 2002

British Library Cataloguing in Publication Data
A catalogue record for this book is available from the British Library

ISBN 0 7506 3668 8

For information on our publications visit our website at www.bh.com/pergamonfl

Typeset by Avocet Typeset, Brill, Aylesbury, Bucks
Printed and bound in Great Britain

Contents

Series overview v
Workbooks in the Institute of Management Opening Learning Programme ix
Links to qualifications xi
Links to other workbooks xii
Introduction xiii

Section 1 Planning and control **1**
Influencing the future 1
Stages in planning 2
Controlling operations 14
Budgets in the planning process 21
Summary 31

Section 2 Financial information **32**
The balance sheet 32
The profit and loss account 43
The cash flow statement 47
Financial ratios 52
Summary 58

Section 3 Looking into the future **59**
The need to produce forecasts 59
Forecasting techniques 63
Summary 72

Section 4 Drawing up a Budget forecast **73**
Identifying the parameters 73
Gathering information 79
Drawing up the budget 88
Presenting your budget forecast 91
Submitting your budget forecast 93
Summary 97

Section 5 Keeping control **98**
Keeping track 98

Monitoring a budget 102
Getting the information 104
Reporting on your budget 107
Evaluation 108
Summary 111

Summary 112
Recommended reading 113
About the Institute of Management 114

Series overview

The Institute of Management Open Learning Programme is a series of workbooks prepared by the Institute of Management and Pergamon Open Learning for managers seeking to develop themselves.

Comprising seventeen open learning workbooks, the programme covers the best of modern management theory and practice, and each workbook provides a range of frameworks and techniques to improve your effectiveness as a manager, thus helping you acquire the knowledge and skill to make you fully competent in your role.

Each workbook is written by an experienced management writer and covers an important management topic or theme. The activities both reinforce learning and help to relate the generic ideas to your individual work context. While coverage of each topic is fully comprehensive, additional reading suggestions and reference sources are given for those who wish to study to a greater depth.

Designed to be practical, stimulating and challenging, the aim of the workbooks is to improve performance at work by benefiting you and your organization. This practical focus is at the heart of the competence based approach that has been adopted by the programme.

The structure of the programme

The design and overall structure of the programme has two main organizing principles, both of which are closely linked to the national standards for management developed by the MCI (Management Charter Initiative).

First, the workbooks are grouped according to the key roles of management.

- Underpinning the management standards are a series of **personal competences** which describe the personal skills required by all managers, which are essential to skill in all the main functional or key role areas.
- **Manage Activities** describes the principles of managing processes and activities, with service to the customer as an essential part of this.
- **Manage Resources** describes the acquisition, control and monitoring of financial and other resources.
- **Manage People** looks at the key skills involved in leadership, developing one's staff and managing their performance.

- **Manage Information** discusses the acquisition, storage and use of information for communication, problem solving and decision making.

In addition, there are three specialized key roles: **Manage Quality, Manage Projects** and **Manage Energy**. The workbooks cover the first two of these. Unlike the four primary key roles above, these are not compulsory for certificate, diploma or S/NVQ requirements, but provide options for the latter.

Together, these key roles provide a comprehensive description of the fundamental principles of management as it applies in any organization – commercial, maintained sector or not-for-profit.

Second, the programme is organized according to **levels of management**, seniority and responsibility.

Level 4 represents first line management. In accredited programmes this is equivalent to S/NVQ Level 4, Certificate in Management or CMS. Level 5 is equivalent to middle/senior management and is accredited at S/NVQ Level 5, Diploma in Management or DMS. There are two S/NVQs at Level 5: Operational Management and Strategic Management. The operations role is focussed internally within an organization on the maintenance of systems and standards of output, whilst the strategic role is focussed on the whole organization, including the external operating environment, and looks at setting directions.

Together, the workbooks cover all the background knowledge you need to have for all units of competence in the MCI standards at Level 4 and Level 5 (apart from the specialized units in the key role Manage Energy). They also provide skills development and opportunities for portfolio building.

For a comprehensive list of workbooks, see page ix. For a comprehensive list of links with the standards, see the *User Guide*.

How to use the programme

The programme is deliberately designed to be flexible and can be used in a variety of ways:

- to update on important management topics and themes, or develop individual skills: as the workbooks are grouped according to themes, it should be easy for you to pick out one that suits your needs
- as part of generic management development programmes: you can choose the modules that fit the themes of the programme

- **as part of, and in support of, accredited competence-based programmes.**

For N/SVQs at both Levels 4 and 5, there are options in the combinations of units that make up the various awards. By using the map provided in the *User Guide*, individuals will be able to select the workbooks appropriate to their specific needs, and their chosen accreditation options. Some of the activities will help you provide evidence for your portfolio; where we think this is the case, we give the relevant reference to the standards.

For Certificate or CMS, Diploma or DMS, individuals should choose modules that not only meet their individual needs but also satisfy the requirements of the delivering body and the awarding body.

You may need help and guidance in these choices, and the *User Guide* sets out the options and advice in much more detail. A fuller description of the potential uses of this material in evidence gathering and portfolio building can also be found in the *User Guide*, as can a detailed description of the contents of each workbook.

Workbooks in the Institute of Management Open Learning Programme

Personal Competences (Levels 4 and 5)

1 *The Influential Manager**
2 *Managing Yourself**

Manage Activities (Level 4)

3 *Understanding Business Process Management*
4 *Customer Focus*

Manage Activities (Level 5)

5 *Getting TQM to Work*
6 *Leading from the Front*
7 *Improving Your Organization's Success*

Manage Resources (Level 4)

8 *Project Management*
9 *Budgeting and Financial Control*

Manage Resources (Level 5)

10 *Effective Financial and Resource Management*

Manage People (Level 4)

1 *The Influential Manager*
2 *Managing Yourself*
11 *Getting the Right People to do the Right Job*
12 *Developing Yourself and Your Staff*
13 *Building a High Performance Team*

Manage People (Level 5)

14 *The New Model Leader*

Manage Information (Level 4)

15 *Making Rational Decisions*
16 *Communication*

Manage Information (Level 5)

17 *Successful Information Management*

Manage Quality (Level 4)

3 *Understanding Business Process Management**
4 *Customer Focus**

Manage Quality (Level 5)

5 *Getting TQM to Work**

Manage Projects (Level 4)

8 *Project Management**

Manage Projects (Level 5)

8 *Project Management**

Support Materials

18 *User Guide*
19 *Mentor Guide*

An asterisk indicates that a particular workbook also contains material suitable for a particular key role or personal competence over and above that where it is principally designated.

Links to qualifications

S/NVQ programmes

This workbook can help candidates to achieve credit and develop skills in the key role Manage Resources at Level 4, and covers the following units and elements:

B3 Manage the use of financial resources	B3.1 Make recommendations for expenditure B3.2 Control expenditure against budgets

Certificate and Diploma programmes

This workbook, together with the other Manage Resources Level 4 workbook *Project Management* covers all of the knowledge required in the key role Manage Resources for Certificate in Management and CMS programmes.

Links to other workbooks

Links to other workbooks

The other workbook in the key role Manage Information at Level 4 is:

8 *Project Management*

And at Level 5:

10 *Effective Financial and Resource Management*

The theme of this workbook is closely associated with:

15 *Making Rational Decisions*

Introduction

Planning and control are closely linked. A plan is useless if you have no control over the way it is carried out. And you cannot control a situation unless you know what it is you are trying to achieve.

Planning and control are actually both part of the same cyclical process:

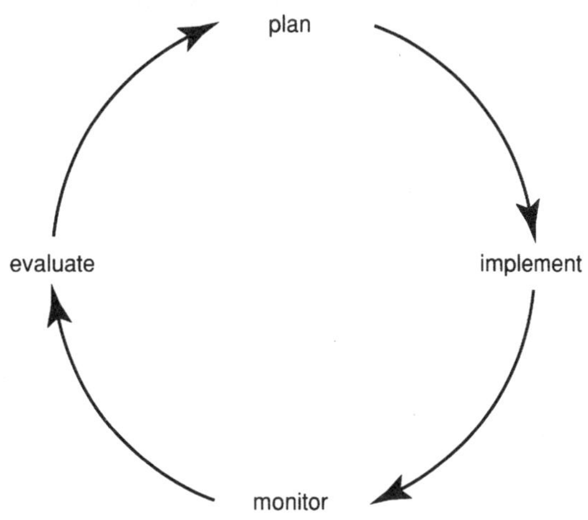

In this first section we will look at the basic steps in business planning and see how an organization decides on its direction, implements this decision at an operational level and monitors progress.

An organization's system of preparing and monitoring budgets fulfils a similar function to a human being's central nervous system. It is the way in which an organization controls its actions and stays alive. In this section we will consider the crucial role that budgeting plays. We will look at some of the problems that can arise if different parts of the process are not properly integrated with each other.

In addition, we will consider the whole question of managing financial resources – how to make a business case, and how to monitor expenditure.

Objectives

By the end of this workbook you should be able to:

- **Understand the importance of business planning at different levels (strategic, division and operating plans) and how controlling resources leads to achieving objectives**

- Apply techniques for financial planning and forecasting, and devise budgets and operational plans
- Implement techniques for financial analysis, monitoring and control
- Construct and communicate a business case

Section I Planning and Control

Influencing the future

Nobody can control the future. However, if we make plans we may at least exert some influence on what happens. Things may not turn out exactly as we had expected, but if we try to think ahead, we are likely to have more control than if we simply react to events.

Planning is something that comes more naturally to some people than others. In everyday life, you may be the sort of person who makes lists of household tasks, books restaurant tables in advance and arranges holidays a year ahead. Or you may be the type of individual who prefers to retain a sense of spontaneity and leave some things to chance. If you come into the second category, you may feel that you are leading a more exciting life than friends who are better organized, but you will probably actually be doing rather less than them. If we don't make plans, the possibilities that are open to us are likely to be greatly reduced.

In business, spontaneity is not an option. There are several reasons for this. First, the consequences of a lack of planning are likely to be much more serious for an organization than they are for an individual. For example, if you fail to plan your income in retirement, you will probably find yourself severely financially restricted when you stop work, but you are unlikely to starve. A business that does not plan where its income will come from in future years faces extinction.

Secondly, it usually takes much longer for an organization to adapt itself to events than it does an individual. If a business is going to make a major change of direction, it needs time to buy premises and plant, design new products and processes and recruit and train new staff.

Thirdly, investors, employees and all the other people who have an interest in an organization expect it to plan for the future. You would not take a job with a company that you thought would go out of business next month. As a supplier, you would not deliver goods to an organization that you thought would be unable to pay your invoice. An investor would not buy shares in a company – and the bank would not give credit – unless the business appeared to be a going concern. In order to maintain their credibility, organizations have to demonstrate a commitment to the future.

Stages in planning

Whether you are a senior manager who is thinking about what your organization will be doing in five years' time, or an ordinary individual thinking about how you will spend your holiday next summer, the planning process follows very similar lines.

CONSIDERING WHAT YOU WANT

The first step is to decide what it is you want to achieve. This decision will be informed by your values and philosophy. If you are planning a holiday, you might have some underlying thoughts about holidays in general:

It's essential to spend some quality time with the family at least once a year.

I need to completely switch off for two weeks.

I'd rather have a cheap holiday and spend any extra money on the house.

Organizations also have values and a philosophy. These may be formalized in a mission statement that is intended to inspire people with a vision of how things could be in the future.

ACTIVITY 1

What would be your personal 'mission statement' when planning a holiday?

What is the mission statement of the organization you work for?

FEEDBACK

Your answers will have identified the foundations on which further decisions can be taken. For example, if you want an intellectually stimulating holiday, you are probably not going to book two weeks lying on a beach in the sun. Similarly, if an organization is committed to ethically sound investments, it is not going to diversify into the tobacco industry.

SETTING OBJECTIVES

The next step is to set some clear objectives. When an organization is planning its own future, some of its objectives will be financial. These may concern its share of the market, the rates of profit it will achieve or perhaps the return on money invested in the organization. An organization may also have non-financial objectives, perhaps concerning the number of people it will employ, the sites it will occupy or the quality standards it will achieve.

Objectives should be:

- *Specific* – so that everyone involved can understand them
- *Measurable* – so that you will know if, or to what extent, you have achieved them
- *Achievable* – based on what you estimate you are likely to be able to do
- *Realistic* – showing an awareness of internal and external factors that may influence you
- *Time-related* – so that you will have a timescale against which to review your progress

ACTIVITY 2

The following objectives come from a small company on a single site to make quality reproduction antique furniture. The company has employed the same six trained crafts people for the last three years. Do the objectives meet the criteria above? If not, what is wrong with them?

1 To develop the mail order side of the business significantly over the next twelve months.

2 To increase sales by 15 per cent.

3 To open workshops in four new locations by the end of next year.

FEEDBACK

1. This seems a reasonable objective to have, but the word 'significantly' is not quantified, so the objective is not measurable.
2. This objective is not time-related.
3. You do not have to have specialized knowledge of the reproduction furniture industry to realize that it is unlikely that a business that only has six trained employees at present could achieve this rate of expansion. It is possible, but again not very likely, that the market could absorb five times as much of the company's products as it does at the moment. This objective is not achievable and probably also unrealistic.

ANALYSING THE CURRENT POSITION

If a friend you are expecting to turn up for dinner telephones and asks, 'How do I get to your house?' you are likely to answer with another question: 'Where are you at the moment?'

When you have decided what you want to achieve, the next step is to take stock of where you are at the present time. An organization which is thinking about where it is going in the future must take a hard look at where it is – and where it is heading if it makes no changes in what it is doing. This involves doing some research into the internal state of the organization and also what is going on in the outside environment.

ACTIVITY 3

Imagine you are a director of the furniture manufacturer featured in the last activity. What kind of information would you need to gather in order to make a forecast about the company's likely situation in two years' time? Think of six types of information you would need.

1
2
3
4
5
6

FEEDBACK

Useful information for the furniture manufacturer to gather might include:

- sales figures for the last few years – and any trends they reveal
- a projection of future profits
- details of how much capital the company has available to invest
- information on exchange rates and the state of the economy in the UK and in overseas markets
- details of new technological processes and the cost of implementing them
- information about the reproduction furniture trade as a whole and about the activities of any competitors
- information on the availability of resources, such as sustainable hardwoods
- any forthcoming legislation or government policies that might affect the organization's activities

---

In Section 2 of this book we will look at ways in which you can analyse the current position of an organization from the financial information it produces. In Section 3 we will consider some methods that businesses use to try to forecast the future.

It is useful to summarize the strengths and weaknesses of an organization, and the opportunities and threats that it faces, in a SWOT analysis.

Here is a SWOT analysis of the furniture company:

Strengths

- a highly skilled workforce making the furniture
- well-motivated employees
- sales growing by ten per cent per year
- a well-known range of products
- reputation for quality
- customer loyalty
- established source of sustainable hardwoods

Weaknesses

- little marketing experience
- time it takes to train new staff
- lack of space in workshops
- relatively high price of products

Opportunities

- growing enthusiasm for our products in the USA in the last two years
- favourable exchange rates

- government grants for training of new employees

Threats

- cut-price competition from companies making inferior quality products

ACTIVITY 4

Without doing any detailed research, can you summarize the strengths, weaknesses, opportunities and threats of your own organization?

Strengths

Weaknesses

Opportunities

Threats

What types of information would you need in order to do this exercise properly?

FEEDBACK

You probably have a general idea of the strengths and weaknesses of your organization and also of the opportunities and threats in the outside environment. Your answer to the second part of the activity is likely to be very similar to your answer to Activity 3, about the furniture company.

IDENTIFYING THE GAPS

The next stage in the planning process is to identify the gaps between where you will be in the future if things continue as they are – and where you want to be. If you were planning your holiday, you might have discovered that the fly-drive holiday across Canada you had set your heart on would cost you £3,000 and that you only had £1,500 available to spend. You could decide to change your objectives and settle on a different form of holiday, or you could move on to the next stage and try to find a strategy to make the trip possible.

Similarly, if you were planning the development of a business, you might decide that the gap between your targets and your forecasts was too wide to bridge, and revise your objectives. Alternatively, you could look for strategies that would enable you to achieve your targets.

CHOOSING A STRATEGY

A strategy is a long-term overall plan. It is not concerned with details, but with the basic method you will use to achieve your objectives. You can read more about business strategy in Workbook 6. Here, we will describe how one strategy model can be used within the planning process.

Ansoff produced a model to describe the strategies for growth that are available to businesses.

	PRODUCTS	
MARKETS	EXISTING	NEW
EXISTING	market consolidation and penetration	product development
NEW	market development	unrelated diversification

Market consolidation and penetration

This is the least risky form of strategy, because the business is working with products and markets with which it is already familiar. There are actually two strategies in this part of the model. *Market consolidation* means defending existing markets against the competition. *Market penetration* means securing a larger share of existing markets.

Market development

Alternatively, a business can take its existing products into new markets. These may be new geographical areas or new market segments.

Product development

Here, the business develops new products for existing markets.

Unrelated diversification

If it chooses this option, the business develops new products for new markets. There is more risk attached to this option than to any of the others, because the business is not using its familiarity with its old markets or its confidence in its products to help it.

ACTIVITY 5

Look back at the SWOT analysis of the furniture business. Which strategy for growth do you think is most appropriate?

- ❑ market consolidation
- ❑ market penetration
- ❑ product development
- ❑ market development
- ❑ unrelated diversification

Why?

FEEDBACK

This company's strengths lie in its products and in the loyalty of its customers. It acknowledges that it is weak in the area of marketing. One option would be to introduce new products to its existing customers. However, it may be facing some dangerous competition from other companies who are selling inferior products at a lower price. It might be a good idea for the business to get some marketing advice and consolidate its markets. It could also get marketing advice on ways in which it could develop other markets for these products.

Generally, Ansoff advised organizations to try to maintain a common thread through their activities, so that effort and resources in one area can support effort and resources in another. He also suggested that companies should select a strategy that exploits their unique competitive advantage and avoids their weaknesses.

Here is what the director of the furniture company decided:

We were very tempted to develop the US market for our products, but in the end we decided it was too risky for us. We would have had to manufacture in the USA, and realized that we would be working in a completely unfamiliar market and would lose control of the area where we are strongest, the quality of our products. We were aware of the dangers of cut-price competition and felt that it was important to consolidate our present markets. But we wanted to go for growth as well. In the end we decided to increase the range of products we sold to our existing market, feeling that this would also consolidate our position with our present customers.

If a business decides to develop one side of its activities, it may have to settle for zero growth, or even retrenchment, in other directions. A business that wants to expand also has to decide whether it will do this by organic growth or by taking over other companies.

It is important to generate a range of strategies for consideration. You may be able to draw upon strategies that your organization has used in the past, or strategies that other organizations have used in similar situations. The business press is a good source of information on what has worked for other businesses.

When a business selects a strategy, it needs to have as clear a picture as possible of the implications of alternative decisions. A useful tool to use at this point is a decision tree, which allows you to assess the probability of various outcomes. (Decision trees are discussed in Workbook 5.) Computer modelling, in which you build 'what if' scenarios, can help you to estimate the financial and other consequences of various strategies.

DESIGNING STRATEGIC, TACTICAL AND OPERATIONAL PLANS

Once you have selected your strategy, it is time to develop your plans in more detail. There are three levels of planning:

- strategic
- tactical
- operational

The strategic plan is the formal statement of the strategy that has been selected. It may not go into much detail, but should state the overall direction in which the organization is going to move.

The tactical plan deals with the medium term. If the strategic plan answers the question: 'What are we going to do?' the tactical plan answers the question: 'How are we going to do it?' It describes the means by which the strategic plan will be put into action.

An operational plan deals with what is going to happen on the ground. In an organizational context, it describes what is going to be achieved on a day-by-day or week-by-week basis.

The following details the three plans of the furniture company:

- **Strategic plan**
  The furniture manufacturer has decided to go ahead with the development of new products for its existing markets.
- **Tactical plan**
  The company asks a well-known furniture designer to come up with some new items to add to the range. It also decides to hire a marketing firm that will help define and promote the company's image for quality. Prototypes of the new designs will be made and the marketing company will do some research to find out which are most popular with customers. The company also decides to monitor sales growth carefully and, when the figures suggest the time is right, expand production by bringing in trainees under a government-supported scheme.
- **Operational plan**
  The workshop is to move from a system where it manufactured to order to a system where it makes for stock. Weekly production targets are set for the workshop. One of the crafts people is put in charge of the new trainees and told to instruct them in the simpler parts of the manufacturing process.

ACTIVITY 6

Think about your own organization. Can you identify an example of each level of plan that you have been involved in implementing? What contribution, if any, did you make to the construction of the plan?

Strategic plan

My contribution

Tactical plan

My contribution

Operational plan

My contribution

FEEDBACK

You probably have quite a lot of input into the operational plans of your organization, especially in the areas where you have direct managerial responsibility, and some input into its tactical plans. Strategic plans are usually the province of senior management.

In the last activity, you may have found it quite difficult to distinguish between the different levels of planning. They are, or at least should be, closely linked. A strategic plan cannot succeed if it depends on an unworkable tactical plan or an impracticable operational plan. Below is an example of a tactical plan that ran into difficulties because it did not reflect operational realities:

First line manager in waste disposal company

One day I came into work and there was a message from the managing director. From next month, the company was not going to pay any overtime but was going to get all the rounds done within the normal working day. Well, fair enough, not a bad idea on paper, but it could only work if I had a complete fleet of vehicles on the road. The problem was that I had two lorries in the yard which I could not afford to send to the garage until the start of the next quarter because I was up to the limit on my maintenance budget. Without those two lorries, I could not rework my routes properly. The result, which from where I stood was completely predictable, was a lot of uncollected rubbish and a lot of unhappy customers.

Most junior managers can give examples of impossible demands that have been put on them by senior management in pursuit of a strategic or tactical plan. And most senior managers can give examples of the unwillingness to adapt to new circumstances of people lower down the organization. This tension between overall strategy and the reality of day-to-day operations is one of the major sources of frustration and dissatisfaction within organizations.

The way to avoid, or at least to minimize, these difficulties is for all planning decisions to be based on a realistic appreciation of what it is possible for the organization, and the people within it, to achieve. This information is assembled by managers who have a genuine understanding of operations and is passed up the organization to senior management.

ACTIVITY 7

Think of a strategic or tactical plan that you found it difficult, or even impossible, to implement.

Now complete this sentence:

I could have implemented this plan easily if only senior management had given me more

FEEDBACK

Your answer may be among this list:

- warning
- time
- skilled staff
- equipment
- money in my budget

In the final analysis, most plans (unless they are completely out of touch with reality) can be implemented if the proper resources are made available. The provision of any resources, including time and skills, has financial implications for the organization.

A plan needs to be based on a realistic idea of what operations will cost and the profit they will generate. This information is usually set out in the form of budgets.

IMPLEMENTING AND MONITORING THE PLANS

The final stage of the planning process is to put the plans into action and monitor what happens. At this point, the function of a budget is to act as a control on how closely the activities are going to plan.

Think back to the individual mentioned earlier in this section who was planning a fly-drive holiday in Canada. Before the holiday began, he made a forecast of how much money he would need to spend each day and the distances he would travel. Once the holiday was underway, he kept a careful record of how much he was spending each day and how far he had travelled and compared this information with his budget and itinerary.

ACTIVITY 8

Imagine that you are the director of the furniture business featured in earlier activities. What information would you need to receive on a regular basis to monitor whether your plans were working?

FEEDBACK

You would be very interested in knowing whether the investments you have made in new designs and marketing advice are proving worth while. You would therefore need to monitor sales figures and the cost to the organization of making these sales. This would include the normal manufacturing costs, the payments you are making to the designer and marketing consultant and anything you are spending on advertising or market research. You also have a plan to use extra money coming into the company to expand your workforce and it would be important to know when you had the cash available to do this. You would also need to keep track of whether production was keeping up with sales. As well as your strategy of product development, you also hoped to consolidate your market share. It could be quite difficult to find out how well you were doing in relation to competing firms, but you might be able to get hold of industry-wide figures and compare your own sales trends with the general picture.

The information you collect on your operations allows you to modify your operational plans to achieve your short-term targets. It also gives you early warning about how your medium- and long-term plans are proceeding, and any elements of them that you may need to look at again.

Director of furniture business

Our original tactic was to increase production by introducing trainees into the workshop. What actually happened was that sales grew much more quickly than we anticipated. Although trainees were a relatively cheap way of increasing the workforce, they did not help us to increase production significantly. We therefore stopped bringing in trainees and employed three experienced carpenters instead.

Controlling operations

From what you have read so far, you will realize that, in order to control a system, you need to:

1. know what it is you are trying to achieve
2. measure the outputs and compare them with your targets

If your outputs match your targets, you can probably assume that your system is working well and you can leave it alone. However, if your outputs do not match your targets, you need to take some remedial action. To do this, you need to:

3. predict the effect of any changes you make to the process
4. correct any deviations from your targets

You can see these four steps in the following case study.

CASE STUDY

1 The editor of a local newspaper which is part of a national group has been set a target of selling 100 000 copies each week.
2 She monitors the number of copies printed each week and the numbers returned unsold by newsagents. These figures tell her that she is only selling 90 000 copies each week.
3 The editor knows she must do something to increase sales. She considers a number of options, including reducing the selling price, including money-off tokens, changing the style of the reporting and developing the classified section of the paper. Her experience of the newspaper trade and knowledge of her readers helps her decide which is the best option.
4 She introduces a new scheme whereby readers can advertise items for less than £30 free of charge.

ACTIVITY 9

Think of a process for which you are responsible. How does this model of control apply to it?

1 What operational targets are you set?

2 How do you monitor outputs and compare them with your targets?

3 How do you know the potential effect of any changes you will make to the process?

4 What do you do to correct deviations from your targets?

FEEDBACK

Managers who are closely involved in operations often have to make decisions on an hour-by-hour or even minute-by-minute basis. They need considerable technical understanding of the processes involved.

When you are controlling operations, you are actually going through a miniature version of the planning process we looked at earlier. Much of the process may happen very quickly and some of it may be automatic to you because you are so familiar with the situation you are working in. However, every time you change an aspect of operations, you are in fact assessing the gap between your targets and the actual situation, assessing various strategies and implementing the one that you predict is most likely to work.

Control systems in organizations are often represented by diagrams such as Figure 1.

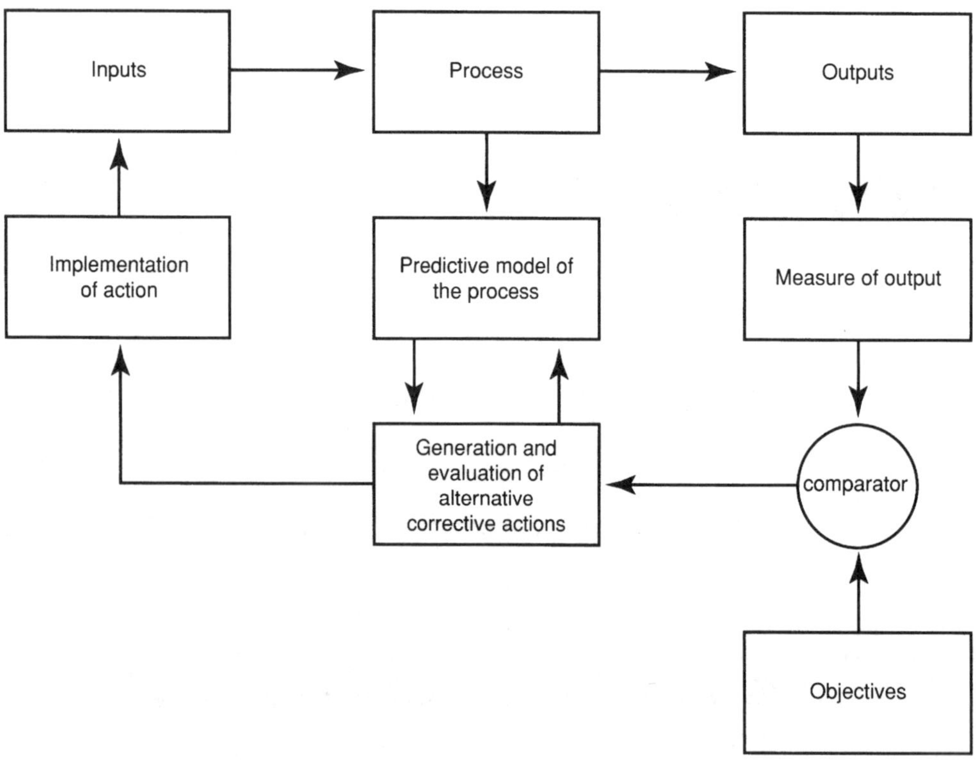

Figure 1 Diagrammatic representation of a control system (from Managing Financial Resources, Michael Broadbent and John Cullen. The Institute of Management Foundation and Butterworth-Heinemann, 1995)

As you can see from Figure 1, it may be necessary to change either the process or the inputs into the process.

CASE STUDY

Dentist

The money we make in the practice depends on the number of people we have registered and the number of treatments we give each week. Our books showed that we were not seeing enough people in the surgery, although patients were queuing up to make appointments. Basically, we had to speed up our treatment. We made two changes to achieve this. First, I spent a lot of money on a system that used a material for fillings that hardened very quickly under a special light gun. We also sent patients out to the waiting room again after they had had their injections, instead of letting them sit in the chair while the anaesthetic took effect. This greatly increased the throughput of patients.

ACTIVITY 10

In the case study you have just read, what changes to inputs and processes does the dentist make?

Inputs

Processes

FEEDBACK

The new equipment would be classified as a change to inputs and the new system for fillings and the revised procedure with patients who have injections would both be classified as changes to processes.

ACTIVITY 11

Now think of an example from your own experience where you modified inputs or the process itself in order to achieve your objectives. Use the framework of Figure 2 to describe what you did.

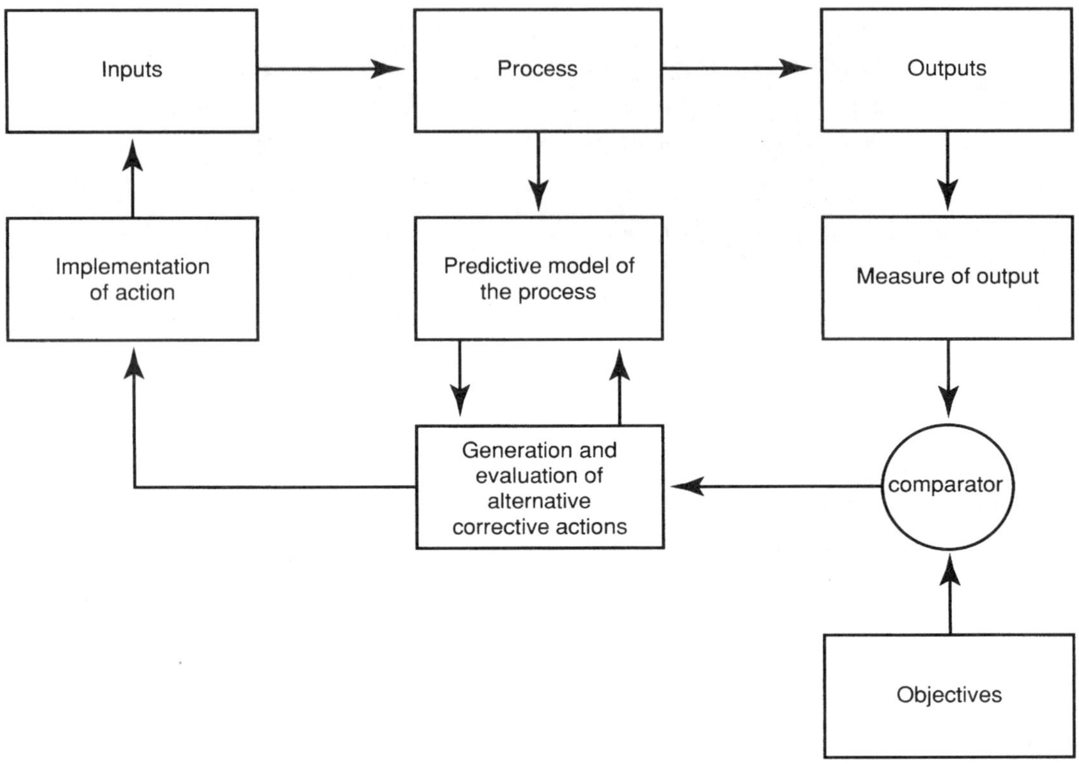

Figure 2 Framework for Activity 11

FEEDBACK

You may have been able to think of an example where you knew exactly what to do in order to bring operations into line with your targets. Or you may have had to try a range of different actions until you found the one that worked. In real life, things are not always as clear cut as they appear in theoretical models.

The model of control you have just been applying is often described in terms of a thermostat on a central heating system. If a specified temperature is not met, the thermostat turns on the fuel supply to the boiler until the room temperature has risen to the required level. There are, however, significant differences between an automatic thermostat and a control system within an organization.

Here are some of the difficulties that you may meet in practice:

- Delay in receiving feedback

  It takes two weeks for sales figures to be compiled by head office. By the time we know how we are performing in relation to the whole group, the situation will have changed.

- Interference with feedback

  Branch managers know that they are expected to reach a certain level of sales each month. It has been known, if they have a particularly good month, for them to carry over some sales to the next month, just to be on the safe side.

- Interference from unavoidable outside events

  Sales of our products always go down when the weather is particularly bad. There's nothing we can do about it. There is therefore no point in changing the system.

- Inappropriate measures of output

  We thought our consultancy was doing well because our order book was full. Actually, we were in deep trouble because we really weren't charging a realistic rate for our services. We were actually making a loss on some jobs.

- Lack of knowledge of the situation

  We knew that we were going wildly over budget. But we were facing a new situation and quite frankly didn't have the faintest idea how to deal with it.

- Interdependency of different systems

  We managed to reduce the number of errors that the clerical staff were making when processing orders, but the extra time this took had a knock-on effect on the despatching system and we got a lot of complaints from customers who were receiving their orders late.

ACTIVITY 12

Think of examples from your own experience where you found it difficult to monitor your activities.

- Delay in receiving feedback
- Interference with feedback
- Interference from unavoidable outside events
- Inappropriate measures of output
- Lack of knowledge of the situation
- Interdependency of different systems
- Other types of difficulty

FEEDBACK

Your experience of what can go wrong with a monitoring and control system can help you devise a more effective system the next time around. Look back at your answers to the activity and note down what you did, or could do in future, to avoid this problem happening again.

In the final section of this book we will take a closer look at methods of financial control.

Budgets in the planning process

Planning and control depend on the circulation of information around the organization. Planning decisions are based on information about what has happened in the past and what it would be possible to do in the future. This information travels up the organizational structure to the senior managers who decide the overall direction of the business. Information about what *should* happen is passed down the organization. Finally, information about what actually *does* happen is passed up to managers who are responsible for operations, tactics or overall strategy.

The information necessary for planning and control can take many forms. As a manager, you may receive (and also produce) written guidelines, policy documents, directives, briefing notes, personal appraisals and reports, all of which are intended to keep your organization's operations in line with its overall strategies and objectives. Very frequently, information related to planning and control is expressed in terms of money and is presented in the form of budget forecasts and budgets.

At this point, it is useful to define the difference between these types of documentation.

- A *budget forecast* is a statement, organized under particular headings, of the expenditure and/or income that is **expected** within a certain period of time.
- A *budget* is a statement, organized under particular headings, of the expenditure and/or income that is **allocated** for a certain period of time.

ACTIVITY 13

Would you classify the following documents as budgets or budget forecasts? Tick the appropriate boxes.

		Budget	Budget forecast
1	You send your manager some figures showing how much you will need to spend to update the IT equipment in your department.	❑	❑
2	Store managers receive details from head office on the level of sales they are expected to achieve in the next six months.	❑	❑

	Budget	Budget forecast
3 A marketing manager receives details of the money which she may spend to advertise a new product, based on estimated sales figures for the product over the next six months.	❑	❑

FEEDBACK

1 is a budget forecast and 2 is a budget. You may have found 3 slightly more difficult, but this is also a budget. Although the amount the marketing manager has available has been calculated using estimated figures, this amount has now been agreed and allocated for this purpose.

Generally, budget forecasts are prepared by those who will spend or generate the money involved. They represent the flow of information up the organizational structure. Budgets give the sanction of senior management to this spending or level of revenue. They represent the flow of information down the structure.

In practice, the two documents may contain exactly the same figures. If a manager has prepared a budget forecast carefully, there may be nothing for senior management to dispute and the forecast will be accepted as the budget to which the manager will work. However, once budget forecasts from several departments are brought together, some rebalancing may be necessary. A department may need to draw up more than one version of a budget forecast before the final budget can be agreed.

TYPES OF BUDGET

Most organizations draw up several different kinds of budget.

Sales budget

All organizations try to forecast their future income. For an organization that makes its money by selling its products or services, the sales budget is therefore a key document. A typical sales budget gives monthly projections for the forthcoming year. If an organization sells products, the budget usually gives the volume of each product (or type of product) that it expects to sell, together with the unit price and the value of sales. So, a publisher's sales budget might include information as shown in Table 1.

Table 1 Sales budget

		January	**February**	**March**
Hamsters for fun	Volume	300	250	250
	Price	3	3	3
	Value	900	750	750
All you need to know about cats	Volume	150	120	100
	Price	7	7	7
	Value	1,050	840	700

In this example, it is clear that a greater volume of sales is expected for the book about hamsters than the book about cats. However, because the unit price of the cat book is higher, the value of the sales will be greater. The publishing company might also find it useful to analyse its sales budget according to the categories of books. It might, for example, look at the expected value of sales from its range of titles about pets and compare it with the value of sales of its books on golf.

An organization that sells services would also be interested in the volume of sales, unit price and value of sales. It would select headings and categories for its sales budget which provided the most useful information to managers. For example, a hotel might measure its sales of accommodation in rooms per night, its restaurant sales in covers, its bar sales in the volume of various drinks sold and the use of its business centre in the number of hours booked.

As the months covered by a budget proceed, actual sales are added to the budget and the variance calculated and recorded. We will look at methods of monitoring budgets in the final section of this book.

Production budget

Any organization which manufactures items for sale needs a production budget. This describes the quantities that will be produced and the costs of producing them. Typically, these costs would include the costs of materials, labour and overheads involved in production. Advertising and any other costs not related directly to production would not be included in this budget. Like the sales budget, the production budget lists the volume, price and value of any items that can be costed in this way. This makes it possible to understand the implications of changes in volume, price and cost.

Capital expenditure budget

This budget gives details of what will be spent on long-term assets, such as land, buildings, vehicles or equipment. These are items that are not used up in the production process.

Departmental budget

Within a large organization, there are usually departments that do not produce anything themselves but which support the areas of the organization that do. These departments often have their own budgets, listing salaries, expenses and other costs.

Master budget

The various budgets described so far are prepared in budget forecast form, usually by the managers responsible for the relevant departments. Senior management then assembles all the information and prepares a master budget.

This contains:

- a cash flow forecast – showing what cash will be coming into the organization, and when it will be coming
- a profit and loss forecast – showing the profit or loss that the organization will be making at the end of the budget period
- a balance sheet forecast – showing what the organization will own (and owe) at the end of the budget period

At the end of the budget period, actual cash flow and profit and loss statements and balance sheets will be prepared. These will tell senior managers, and other interested parties such as banks, shareholders and the Inland Revenue, how well the organization is doing. In the next section of this book we will look at the kind of information they can reveal.

In their forecast form, the cash flow statement, profit and loss statement and balance sheet allow senior management to explore the implications of the various budget forecasts. The master budget may indicate that changes have to be made to these forecasts. For example, expected profits may not be high enough to support the existing level of spending on administration. Capital projects, such as extending premises, may have to be postponed until sufficient cash has been received from customers. It may be advantageous to buy more stock in advance at a cheaper rate and so be able to reduce retail prices and increase sales. Once decisions of this kind have been taken, adjustments can be made to the individual budget forecasts and the final budgets produced.

Catering manager in large office

I told my manager what I wanted to spend in the next six months. But when the sales forecast came in, the company decided that things were not looking good and said that there had to be 15 per cent cuts across all departments, so it was back to the drawing board.

Sales manager in publishing company

I based my forecast of sales on what we had managed in the same quarter of the previous year. However, the managing director told me that he was prepared to make an investment in order to improve sales and was going to agree a large increase to the advertising budget. He asked me to re-work the figures, with the assumption that sales of certain titles would rise accordingly.

THE BUDGET PERIOD

Organizations usually take a long-term approach to budgeting. Capital projects often last for longer than one year and it is necessary to plan to have adequate funds available to finance them for the entire duration of the project.

The typical budget period is five years, although this can vary according to the needs of the individual organization. Obviously, an organization which needs to plan capital expenditure ten years into the future will need to budget for that period, while an organization with less demanding capital expenditure needs will be able to adopt a shorter planning horizon.

The usual approach to long-term budgeting is to plan the next year's budget in detail, with the second year's budget in rather less detail and the third and later years' budgets in little more than outline. A year later, each year's budget is reviewed and updated in the light of events that have occurred during the year and a new final year's budget is added to the end of the budget period.

Budgets are not just prepared for complete years, but are divided into periods of either months or weeks. There are two main reasons for this.

First, flows of profit and cash are usually not constant during the year. An annual budget may show that the organization has sufficient cash coming in, but this may hide a part of the year when the organization is running a cash deficit. Dividing the year into periods of a month is more likely to reveal these short-term trends and give a greater degree of control.

Secondly, the budget is used as a yardstick for assessing actual performance during the year. Dividing the year into shorter periods enables trends to be spotted more quickly and makes it easier to take corrective action before the situation gets out of hand.

ACTIVITY 14

What budget information do you have to supply on a yearly basis?

What budget information do you have to supply on a monthly basis?

What information, if any, do you have to supply more frequently?

FEEDBACK

Developments in information technology have made it possible to monitor activities on a much more frequent basis. Reports can be compiled automatically which would once have taken hours or even days of a manager's time. Geographical distance is also no longer a barrier to the transmission of information.

As it becomes easier to produce data, many organizations are finding that they are suffering from information overload. Too much information can be time-consuming to analyse and can actually be counter-productive in its effect. Many managers report that they find they feel the need to have more and more information before they are able to take simple decisions. Financial information, like other forms of data, needs to be gathered and used with care.

WHAT DO BUDGETS DO?

Budgets provide the essential information that the senior management of an organization needs to plan and control activities. They have several other benefits, too.

Planning

The act of putting together a budget helps everyone involved to look ahead.

Office supervisor
My line manager was working on the departmental budget. He asked me to estimate what we'd need to spend on stationery in the next twelve months. I telephoned our usual supplier who warned me that they were going to put their prices up by ten per cent in a few weeks. We therefore made sure that we put a large order in before the price rise came into effect.

Personnel manager
I was asked to put forward some figures for recruitment advertising to go into the budget. I did some research on the relative cost of advertising and the current circulation figures for the various newspapers we could advertise in. I was surprised to find that one regional paper, which we'd never actually used in the past, had just the right readership profile and was significantly cheaper than the local paper we usually advertised in.

Committing yourself to a budget can help to concentrate the mind. You may be able to avoid problems, and discover opportunities, that you might otherwise have missed. When you have to explain and justify your figures, you may also find that there are more effective ways to do things.

Co-ordination and clarity

Budgets help different parts of a business to understand the significance to the organization as a whole of what they do. This can be motivating to individual members of staff and can increase efficiency.

Hotel manager
There is a clear relationship between the number of repeat customers we get in our hotels and our level of profit. It costs much more to find a new customer than to keep an existing one. I explain this to all our staff.

Control

A budget provides a yardstick against which to measure your activities. It can help you to avoid extravagant spending and to ration your resources.

Office manager
When we work out how much the photocopier is going to cost to use, we base this figure on an average of 500 copies being made each day. I check the counter once a week and, if necessary, have a word with the people responsible. Some people assume

that because the photocopier is there, it doesn't cost anything. By keeping a regular check on things, I manage to stop staff getting into bad habits.

Incentives

A budget is a statement of what is expected of people. It can be motivating to achieve this target – and even better if you manage to improve on it.

ACTIVITY 15

You have just read about the benefits that budgets can bring. Can you think of any disadvantages of preparing or working with a budget?

FEEDBACK

The preparation and monitoring of budgets can be time-consuming. It is therefore important that all the information gathered and analysed is actually useful. Another potential disadvantage is that a budget can set artificial or unnecessary limits on activity. For example, if a department knows that £1,000 has been allocated to the purchase of new software in a particular year, it is very likely to buy software to this value, even if some of the items bought are not strictly necessary. Similarly, if a store knows that it is expected to sell £6,000 worth of goods in a week, it may relax its sales efforts once this target has been reached.

RESPONSIBILITY CENTRES

Within an organization, several kinds of financial responsibility may be held by managers:

- in a *cost centre*, managers are responsible for what they spend
- in a *revenue centre*, managers are responsible for the revenue they bring in
- in a *profit centre*, managers are responsible for costs and revenue

The result of separating responsibility for costs and revenue can be short-sighted decision making. You can probably think of some examples that are similar to the following:

We had a manager in charge of the post room who insisted on saving money by using second class post to send out brochures which had been requested by phone. This was a false economy, because people who phoned for our catalogues usually rang other companies as well. If our catalogue didn't arrive the next day, the chances of making a sale were greatly reduced.

I once had a manager who liked to keep all his regular customers happy by inviting them to the company's hospitality tent at sporting fixtures. This entertainment didn't come out of his budget and the amount it cost the firm was way in excess of the profits that these customers generated.

If the responsibility for costs and revenue is combined in one area, decisions of this kind are much less likely to occur.

In recent years, there has been a tendency to introduce the idea of profit into organizations, and parts of organizations, which previously saw themselves only as cost centres. For example, now that schools are locally managed, they are able to decide how they will spend large parts of their budgets.

Primary headteacher

The money we receive from the local authority is based on the number of pupils in the school. We had enough money to pay for seven teachers, each teaching a class of 28 pupils. We had a suggestion from one of the governors, who was very keen on IT, that we could cut down to six teachers (and six classes) and spend the money saved on state-of-the-art computers in every classroom. This was an interesting idea, but we thought that small class sizes would be more attractive to potential parents and therefore decided to keep the seven teachers.

A purchaser-provider split has been introduced into the National Health Service. Hospitals, which were once regarded as cost centres, now sell their services to health authorities on a contract basis. GP fundholders are able to decide how they will spend their budgets to the best advantage of their patients. Within many public sector organizations, support departments have to tender for the work they would once have been given automatically, competing against commercial companies.

Traditionally, when businesses calculated what it cost them to produce goods and services for sale, they spread indirect costs such as administration and storage across everything that they sold. Indirect costs were apportioned in a fairly arbitrary manner, based on the number of machine hours a particular item took to make, or the floor area that a certain activity occupied. In recent years, there has been a move away from absorption costing of this kind towards activity based costing, in which the indirect costs charged to a particular item bear a much closer relation to the actual costs involved. (We will explore methods of costing in more detail later in this book.)

The effect of these changes has been to turn cost centres into profit centres – or at least to make these centres much more conscious of the implications for profit of what they are doing. One positive consequence is that budgets are likely to be more realistic than they perhaps were in the past. If you are responsible for both costs and revenue, you are unlikely to inflate your costs unnecessarily or to miss opportunities for extra profit. However, the necessity to balance budgets at the level of operations has also led to situations where individuals (such as teachers or nurses) who might be better occupied concentrating on their professional work are obliged to spend more time on administration.

As you can see, the way an organization controls its internal finances can have a far-reaching effect on the activities and priorities of its staff.

ACTIVITY 16

B3.1, B3.2

Conclude your work on this section by considering the role that budgets play in your own organization's system of planning and control. Describe the process by which your own budget is prepared and agreed, and comment on its advantages and disadvantages. How much say do you have in your budget? Would you be able to do your job more effectively if you had more (or less) responsibility in this area?

FEEDBACK

This activity may have revealed some parts of your organization's financial planning and control systems that are beyond your direct experience and which you do not understand. If so, make a note of these areas now. Check back on these points from time to time as you work through the book. Hopefully, you will find that some of your questions have been answered.

Summary

Now that you have finished this section you should be able to:

- describe the stages in the planning process
- recognize various strategies used by organizations
- distinguish between strategic, tactical and operational plans
- apply a model of the control process to your own activities
- recognize obstacles to effective monitoring
- define budgets and budget forecasts
- describe several types of budget
- outline the process of preparing a budget
- describe budget periods
- describe the benefits and potential drawbacks of budgeting

Section 2 Financial Information

The aim of this section is to enable you to read financial statements with understanding. You will see how simple balance sheets, profit and loss accounts and cash flow statements are built up and the kind of information that these documents can tell us about an organization.

If you are already familiar with the style and content of company accounts, you will be able to move through this section very quickly. However, for many non-financial managers, the balance sheet, profit and loss account and cash flow statement retain an air of mystery. In this section we will explain the very simple principles on which company accounts are based and attempt to dispel some of the mystification. By the end, you should have the ability to tackle these statements with much more confidence.

If you are preparing or presenting a budget, you need an understanding of financial statements. This is because everything in your budget will have impact on the forecast balance sheet, profit and loss account and cash flow statement that make up the master budget. You will be able to use the insights you gain in this section to prepare budgets that reflect the financial situation and priorities of your organization.

The balance sheet

We often think of a company being an entity in its own right; it owns things and has financial obligations. You may use a 'company car' or say, 'The company owes me £15 for the taxi I took to the meeting.' But, in the final analysis, it is people, not companies, who own things. A company is only a set of financial and legal arrangements that allows people to invest money in its activities and receive profits. All of a company's assets are paid for by money that has been borrowed or by funds that have been invested by its owners or shareholders. And any profit made by the company belongs, once debts have been paid, to the owners or shareholders. This is as true of a small greengrocer's shop as it is of a multinational organization.

A balance sheet is a statement of a company's assets and the claims people have on the company. These two figures always balance each other exactly. The relationship between assets and claims can be written like this:

Assets = Claims

Assets include buildings, plant and machinery, stocks of raw material and finished goods and investments. There are two types of claim on a company. Liabilities are debts to banks, suppliers and other creditors. Shareholders' equity is money that has been invested in the company by shareholders or has been accumulated by the company and which belongs to the owners or shareholders. So, the equation can be written like this:

Assets = Liabilities + Shareholders' equity

This is the balance sheet equation. The whole structure of business accounting is based on this simple principle.

ACTIVITY 17

A company buys a building for £100 000. It pays for this with £40 000 profit it has accumulated and makes up the difference with a bank loan of £60 000.

Fill in the figures to show how the balance sheet equation works for this transaction.

Assets	=	Liabilities	+	Shareholders' equity
£	=	£	+	£

FEEDBACK

In this situation, the building is an asset, the bank loan is a liability and the profit forms part of the shareholders' equity.

£100 000 = £60 000 + £40 000

Every time a company makes a financial transaction of any kind, an adjustment is made to each side of the balance sheet equation. It is not necessary to draw up a new balance sheet every time, although it would be quite possible to do so. A company normally draws up a balance sheet once a year on a date known as the 'Accounting Reference Date' or more commonly, the 'Year End'.

A good way to understand how a balance sheet works is to see how different kinds of transactions are recorded on it. We will arrange the information in a different way from the format that is normally used for balance sheets in the UK because this makes it easier to see what is happening.

We begin with an empty chart, which shows the assets on one side of the equation and the liabilities and capital on the other. These two sides must always equal each other.

Assets	**£**	**Liabilities and shareholders' equity**	**£**

We will build up a balance sheet for PC Servicing Ltd, a small computer servicing company that has just been set up. The first event that takes place is that the shareholders pay £10 000 into the company. Now the company has an asset of £10 000 cash in its bank account and an equal claim on it from the shareholders.

Assets	**£**	**Liabilities and shareholders' equity**	**£**
Cash	10 000	Share capital	10 000

The company buys a set of specialist repair manuals, costing £75, by cheque. Now the balance sheet looks like this:

Assets	**£**	**Liabilities and shareholder's equity**	**£**
Fixed assets			
Manuals	75		
Current assets			
Cash	9 925	Share capital	10 000

As you can see, the cash in the bank has gone down by £75. The shareholders' equity remains unchanged. We have also divided the assets into two categories. *Fixed assets* are items that are used by the company on a long-term basis and which it does not trade in. *Current assets* are cash and items that the company sells or would expect to use up within a year.

ACTIVITY 18

Would you classify the following as fixed or current assets? Tick the boxes.

		Fixed asset	Current asset
1	Freehold and leasehold land	❑	❑
2	Investments	❑	❑
3	Buildings	❑	❑
4	Plant and equipment	❑	❑
5	Stocks of raw materials	❑	❑
6	Stocks of finished goods for sale	❑	❑
7	Fixtures and fittings	❑	❑
8	Cash and bank balances	❑	❑
9	Money owed to the company	❑	❑
10	Stocks of stationery	❑	❑
11	Motor vehicles	❑	❑
12	Prepayments made to suppliers	❑	❑

FEEDBACK

Items 1, 3, 4, 7 and 11 are fixed assets. All the rest are current assets.

Liabilities are also classified in a similar way. They are described as long-term or current. We will now return to the balance sheet of PC Servicing Ltd.

ACTIVITY 19

Next, the company buys specialist tools worth £250, again by cheque. Amend the balance sheet to show the effect of this transaction.

Assets	£	**Liabilities and shareholders' equity**	£
Fixed assets		*Current liabilities*	
Manuals	75		
Current assets			
Cash	9925	Share capital	10 000

FEEDBACK

This is exactly the same kind of the transaction as the purchase of the manuals. You should have deducted £250 from the cash figure and added another fixed asset to the list.

Assets		**Liabilities and shareholders' equity**	**£**
Fixed assets			
Manuals	75		
Tools	250		
Current assets			
Cash	9675	Share capital	10 000

The next transaction is slightly more complicated. The company buys 100 electronic circuit boards for £900 on three months' credit. Since the circuit boards have been purchased with a view to selling them in the business, they are therefore stock (a current asset). They have been purchased on credit. A cheque has not been written out and the bank balance is not affected. However, it is necessary to make another entry on the balance sheet so that the two sides still balance. This is done by including a creditor (a current liability) for the sum of £900.

Assets	3	**Liabilities and shareholders' equity**	3
Fixed assets		*Current liabilities*	
Manuals	75		
Tools	250	Creditors	900
Current assets			
Stock	900		
Cash	9675	Share capital	10 000

Notice that the stock is included on the balance sheet at the price that the company paid for it, even though it is expected to sell at a profit. This is known as the historic cost principle.

ACTIVITY 20

Next, the company sells ten of its 100 circuit boards at £15 each. There are three changes to be made to the balance sheet. Two of these are on the assets side. What changes would you make to:

1 Cash

2 Stock

3 A new category, retained profit, is created on the liabilities and capital side. What figure should go in here?

FEEDBACK

You should have added £150 to the cash figure. You might have been tempted to subtract this same amount from the stock figure, but remember that stock is valued at the amount that it cost the company. You should have subtracted only £90, one-tenth of £900, from the stock. The asset side of the balance sheet is now £60 higher than it was before the transaction. This £60 is profit that the company has made.

Assets	£	**Liabilities and shareholders' equity**	£
Fixed assets		*Current liabilities*	
Manuals	75		
Tools	250	Creditors	900
Current assets			
Stock	810	Retained profit	60
Cash	9825	Share capital	10 000

ACTIVITY 21

Next, the company services the computer system in a local office and puts in an invoice for £300, to be paid in thirty days. A new category of trade debtors is added to the asset side, with an entry of £300. How would you balance the equation?

FEEDBACK

Nothing has been taken away from the assets of the company by this transaction, so the balancing entry must be made on the other side of equation. The correct answer here is to add £300 to the retained profit.

Assets	£	**Liabilities and shareholder's equity**	£
Fixed assets		*Current liabilities*	
Manuals	75		
Tools	250	Creditors	900
Current assets			
Stock	810		
Trade debtors	300	Retained profit	360
Cash	9825	Share capital	10 000

You will notice that the amount of £300 has to go into the accounts at the time at which it was invoiced, and not when the money is actually received. This is because of the principle of accruals. There are four fundamental accounting concepts that you should be aware of:

1 *The going concern concept* – which assumes that the company will remain in business. Items are valued on the basis of their original cost to the company (minus depreciation, in some cases) rather than on the basis of what they would be worth if the company was wound up.
2 *The accruals concept* – which recognizes sales revenue when a product is sold, rather than when the proceeds of the sale are received, matches the sales revenue with the cost of producing or purchasing what has been sold

and attaches business expenses to the period to which they relate, rather than to the period in which they were paid.

3 *The consistency concept* – which requires consistent treatment of similar items both within a given accounting period and from one accounting period to another. If, for some reason, it is necessary to adopt a different approach to a particular item, then this concept requires that this change is disclosed in the financial statements.
4 *The prudence concept* – which requires a conservative approach, not anticipating profits before they are realized and making proper provision for all known losses at the earliest possible time.

Every time a transaction is recorded on the balance sheet, one or more further entries must be made to ensure that the equation still balances. See if you can decide how the following transactions (Activity 22) would be recorded.

ACTIVITY 22

1 Buy a second-hand van by cheque for £3000

2 Pay £200 repair costs on the van in cash

3 Receive the £300 already invoiced for servicing the computers

FEEDBACK

1 The first transaction is simple. You should have included another fixed asset of £3000 and reduced the cash by the same amount.
2 This repair bill comes out of the bank account. You may have considered balancing this item by increasing the value of the van by £200, but this would not have been correct. (Remember the principle of historic cost.) This transaction affects the profits of the company and you should have reduced the retained profit figure by £200.
3 The cash figure goes up by £300 and the trade debtors figure is reduced to zero.

Now the balance sheet looks like this:

Assets	£	Liabilities and shareholders' equity	£
Fixed assets		*Current liabilities*	
Van	3000	Creditors	900
Manuals	75		
Tools	250		
Current assets			
Stock	810		
Trade debtors	–	Retained profit	160
Cash	6925	Share capital	10 000

VERTICAL FORMAT BALANCE SHEETS

So far, we have presented the balance sheet in a horizontal format, with the assets and claims side by side. This format makes it simple to check that the two sides always balance each other. However, in the UK, the same information is presented in a different way, using a vertical format. Assets are listed first, followed by liabilities. Liabilities are deducted from assets to give a figure known as net assets. At the bottom of the balance sheet, shareholders' equity is listed.

Here is what a balance sheet looks like in a vertical format:

PC Servicing Ltd
Balance sheet

		£
Net assets		
Fixed assets		x
Current assets		
Stock	x	
Prepayments	x	
Trade debtors	x	
Cash	x	
		x
Current liabilities		
Trade creditors	(x)	
Accruals	(x)	
Tax payable	(x)	
Dividends	(x)	
		(x)
Long-term liabilities		(x)
Net assets		x
Shareholders' equity		
Share capital	x	
Retained profit	x	
Total		x

There are a few items on this balance sheet that we have not described yet. Prepayments are payments for assets that have been made in advance of receiving goods or services. They count as an asset, because the company is owed something. They are balanced by a corresponding entry deducted from the cash figure. Accruals are costs associated with making sales that the company knows it will have to pay, but which it has not yet paid. It is important to include them in the balance sheet so that the true cost of making sales can be calculated. Tax is estimated in advance and added to the balance sheet. Tax reduces the retained profit of the company. Dividends are payments made to shareholders to reward them for their investment in the company. They are balanced by taking an equal amount of the retained profit.

ACTIVITY 23

What figure on the balance sheet would you expect to be the same as the figure for shareholders' equity?

FEEDBACK

The balance sheet equation tells us that:

Assets = Liabilities + Shareholders' equity

Therefore:

Shareholders' equity = Assets – Liabilities

You also know that:

Assets – Liabilities = Net assets

So:

Net assets = Shareholders' equity

ACTIVITY 24

Prepare the balance sheet for PC Servicing Ltd using the vertical format.

PC Servicing Ltd
Balance sheet

		£
Net assets		
Fixed assets		
Current assets		
Current liabilities		
Long-term liabilities		
Net assets		
Shareholders' equity		
Total		

Your balance sheet should look like this:

PC Servicing Ltd
Balance sheet

		£
Net assets		
Fixed assets		3325
Current assets		
Stock	810	
Cash	6925	
		7735
Current liabilities		
Trade creditors	(900)	
		(900)
Long-term liabilities		(–)
Net assets		10 160
Shareholders' equity		
Share capital	10 000	
Retained profit	160	
Total		10 160

WHAT A BALANCE SHEET CAN'T TELL YOU

If you were to set up a camera at one end of the garden and take a photograph, the resulting picture would record everything that was in the garden at a particular moment in time. If you were to take another picture the next day, this photograph would probably look much the same, but there could be some differences. For example, the grass may have been mown or someone may have picked the flowers.

Both pictures would be an accurate record of everything that was in the garden, but they would only be a record of the moment in time at which you took the photographs.

A balance sheet is much the same. It is a 'snapshot' of a company's situation at one specific point in time. However, things can move rapidly in business and a balance sheet drawn up one day can differ dramatically from a balance sheet drawn up one day earlier or later.

Another limitation of the balance sheet is that assets are shown at their historic cost, at the price that was originally paid for them, less depreciation. If a company has money invested in buildings or land that were bought some years ago, the figure that appears on the balance sheet can be very misleading. More seriously, the balance sheet does not explain *how* a company came to achieve its retained profits. In order to understand this, you need to look at the profit and loss account.

The profit and loss account

The balance sheet, as you have seen, records a company's situation at a particular moment in time. The profit and loss account records the operations of the company for a period of time, usually for a whole year. A profit and loss account contains the following information:

- *Sales revenue* – the money due from selling goods and services
- *Cost of sales* – any costs and expenses, such as the cost of raw materials, which can be directly assigned to goods and services that are sold
- *Gross profit* – the figure obtained by subtracting the cost of sales from the sales revenue
- *Operating expenses* – any expenses that have been incurred in the operation of the business and cannot be directly assigned to the sales of goods and services. Examples could include administration and advertising
- *Operating profit* – the figure obtained by deducting the operating expenses from the gross profit
- *Loan interest payable* – this figure needs to be deducted because it reduces the amount of profit that the company has made for tax purposes

- *Profit before tax* – the figure obtained by deducting any loan interest from the operating profit
- *Tax payable* – the amount the Inland Revenue will expect to receive
- *Profit after tax* – the figure obtained by deducting the tax payable from the profit before tax
- *Dividend payable* – the amount that is paid to shareholders to reward them for their investment in the company
- *Retained profit* – the amount left after deducting dividends from profit after tax that is available to be reinvested in the company

ACTIVITY 25

Use the framework outlined below to draw up a profit and loss account for a company from the following information:

- Purchased raw materials for £10 000
- Sold finished goods for £40 000
- Spent £4000 on manufacturing expenses
- Spent £2000 on administration
- Spent £3000 on advertising
- Paid loan interest of £1000
- Paid tax at 25 per cent
- Paid a total dividend to shareholders of £500

Profit and loss account

		£
Sales		
Cost of sales		
Raw materials		
Manufacturing expenses		
Gross profit		
Operating expenses		
Administration		
Advertising		
Operating profit		
Interest payable		
Profit before tax		
Tax payable		
Profit after tax		
Dividend payable		
Retained profit		

FEEDBACK

Your profit and loss account should look like this:

Profit and loss account

		£
Sales		40 000
Cost of sales		
Raw materials	(10 000)	
Manufacturing expenses	(4000)	
		(14 000)
Gross profit		26 000
Operating expenses		
Administration	(2000)	
Advertising	(3000)	
		(5000)
Operating profit		21 000
Interest payable		(1000)
Profit before tax		20 000
Tax payable		(5000)
Profit after tax		15 000
Dividend payable		(500)
Retained profit		(14 500)

A profit and loss account explains how a company achieved its retained profit figure. It concentrates on the operating activities and does not tell you anything about the buying or selling of assets or the amount of cash that the company has available.

ACTIVITY 26

Draw up a profit and loss account to show how PC Servicing Ltd achieved its retained profit figure of £160. Use a similar format as illustrated in Activity 25. You can assume that the company paid no tax or dividends in this period.

FEEDBACK

The profit and loss account for PC Servicing Ltd looks like this:

PC Servicing Ltd
Profit and loss account

		£
Sales	150	
	300	
		450
Cost of sales		
Materials	(90)	(90)
Gross profit		360
Operating expenses		
Repairs	(200)	
		(200)
Operating profit		160
Interest payable		–
Profit before tax		160
Tax payable		–
Profit after tax		–
Dividend payable		–
Retained profit		160

We will use this profit and loss statement again in the next part of the section.

The cash flow statement

Companies that have healthy profit and loss accounts can still be in deep trouble because they have a shortage of cash.

ACTIVITY 27

Here is a summary of the transactions of PC Servicing Ltd, whose balance sheet you built up earlier. Tick any of these transactions that affected the amount of cash that the company had.

1. Shareholders pay in £10 000 ❑
2. Buy manuals with cheque (£75) ❑
3. Buy tools with cheque (£250) ❑
4. Buy circuit boards on credit (£900) ❑
5. Sell ten circuit boards for cash (£150) ❑
6. Service computers on credit (£300) ❑
7. Buy van with cheque (£3000) ❑
8. Pay cash for repairs to van (£200) ❑
9. Receive payment for servicing computers (£300) ❑

FEEDBACK

You should have ticked all of the transactions except 4 and 6.

ACTIVITY 28

What is the cumulative effect of these seven transactions on the company's cash?

FEEDBACK

At the end of the period, the company's cash has gone up from zero to £6925.

This change in the company's cash needs to be explained in the accounts. The profit and loss account does not tell us about the money actually spent or received by the company. It excludes information about fixed assets that were bought or sold and does not tell us about loans that were taken out. Transactions like these could have a very significant effect on the company, but they would not be described on the profit and loss account.

It is the role of the cash flow statement to explain the change in a company's cash situation. One way in which this could be done would be to list all the transactions that affect cash and look at their impact, very much as you did in the last two activities. In practice, the cash flow statement adopts a slightly different approach. The cash flow statement takes the figure for operating profit, as given on the profit and loss account, and explains why this is different from the change in the amount of cash that a company has. The information on a cash flow statement is organized under several headings. We will go through them and explain what they all cover.

Operating activities

- *Operating profit* – as given in the profit and loss account. This is the base figure that the statement will reconcile with the change in the cash flow.
  Depreciation – this will have been included as an operating expense in the profit and loss account, but will not have affected the company's cash. Depreciation is added back.
- *Increase in trade debtors* – these are the people who owe the company money. Their payments will have been counted towards sales, but will not have increased the cash that the company holds. This figure is deducted.
- *Increase in stock* – any stock that has not been sold will not affect profit, but it will have required cash to be spent. The amount is deducted from the operating profit figure. If stock was bought on credit, not cash, this adjustment is still made, along with a compensating entry that we will describe in a moment.
- *Increase in prepayments* – these affect cash, but not profits. The amount is deducted.
- *Increase in trade creditors* – these are people to whom the company owes money. The profit has been worked out as if payments to these creditors have been made, although they have not yet had their impact on the cash flow. This figure is added to the operating profit.
- *Increase in accruals* – these are other payments connected with the operating activities that have been counted as an expense but not yet paid. They are treated in the same way as the increase in trade creditors and added back.

Investing activities

This covers the buying and selling of fixed assets. Assets that have been purchased are deducted and assets that have been sold are added.

Servicing of finance

This section deals with loan interest and any other payments that are necessary to maintain the company's sources of finance. Loan interest is deducted, because it has had an impact on the cash flow, but not on the operating profit. Dividends are treated in a similar way. (If you look back at the profit and loss account, you will see that these items are deducted after the operating profit has been calculated.)

Taxation

This needs to be deducted, because it will have affected the cash flow but not the operating profit.

Financing

This section, which should not be confused with the earlier part of the statement that deals with **servicing** of finance, includes money that has come into the business from loans or the issuing of shares. The cash flow will have been increased by this amount, which therefore needs to be added to the figure for operating profit.

ACTIVITY 29

Now try to prepare a cash flow statement for PC Servicing Ltd. Use the following framework to help, although you will not need to use all the headings.

PC Servicing Ltd
Cash flow statement

	£
Operating activities	
Operating profit	
Depreciation	
Increase in trade debtors	
Increase in stock	
Increase in prepayments	
Increase in trade creditors	
Increase in accruals	
Investing activities	
Servicing of finance	
Taxation	
Financing	
Shares issued	
Net change in cash balance	

FEEDBACK

If your cash flow statement produced a net change in cash balance of £6925, you probably got the intermediate working right. Check the details with the answer below.

PC Servicing Ltd
Cash flow statement

		£
Operating activities		
Operating profit	160	
Depreciation	–	
Increase in trade debtors	–	
Increase in stock	(810)	
Increase in prepayments	–	
Increase in trade creditors	900	
Increase in accruals	–	
		250
Investing activities		
Purchase of fixed assets	(3325)	(3075)
Servicing of finance	–	(3075)
Taxation	–	(3075)
Financing		
Shares issued	10 000	
Net change in cash balance		6925

If you have worked through all the activities in this section, you should now have a sound grasp of the basics of company accounts. We will now go on to look at what the figures in these statements can tell us.

Financial ratios

Two companies both make an operating profit of £100 000 in a particular year. However, the first of these companies is owned and run by a single person who has invested £200 000 of her own money in the business. The second company is a large organization in which £1 000 000 has been invested. The first company is clearly doing much better than the second one. One way to describe exactly how much better the first company is doing would be to divide the profits by the amount of capital invested in the companies and express the result as a percentage:

$$\frac{£100\ 000}{£200\ 000} = 50 \text{ per cent}$$

$$\frac{£100\ 000}{£1\ 000\ 000} = 10 \text{ per cent}$$

This is an example of one of the many financial ratios that can be calculated from company accounts to highlight significant information. There are three broad types of financial ratio:

- performance measures
- financial status measures
- investment measures

We will look at each in turn.

PERFORMANCE MEASURES

These ratios assess how a company is being run. The most common measure is return on capital employed, known as ROCE. Companies use a mixture of shareholders' funds and long-term loans to finance their operations. This measure shows how well a company's management has used these funds to generate profit.

The ratio is calculated by taking the earnings before tax and interest on long-term loans and dividing by the total capital employed. (This is what we did at the beginning of our discussion of financial ratios.) We have not discussed the term 'capital employed' yet. It is the figure you get if you add together the shareholders' equity, long-term loans and the tax that the company pays.

ACTIVITY 30

Check you understand the principle by working out the ROCE for a company that has an operating profit of £30 000, shareholders' capital of £35 000, a long-term loan of £5000 and pays tax of £5000.

FEEDBACK

$$\text{ROCE} = \frac{\text{operating profit}}{\text{total capital employed}}$$

$$\frac{£30\ 000}{£45\ 000} = 66 \text{ per cent}$$

It is sometimes helpful to measure how effectively management has used the funds provided by shareholders alone, that is, disregarding the long-term loans. This measure is called return on equity (ROE) and is calculated by taking the earnings after tax and dividing by the shareholders' funds.

ACTIVITY 31

If a company had profits after tax of £475 000 and shareholders' equity of £1 500 000, what would the ROE be? Give your answer as a percentage.

FEEDBACK

$$\text{ROE} = \frac{\text{profit after tax}}{\text{shareholders' funds}}$$

$$\frac{£475\ 000}{£1\ 500\ 000} = 31.7 \text{ per cent}$$

FINANCIAL STATUS MEASURES

These ratios help us assess the financial strength of a company. One of the key measures is the debt ratio, which compares the amount of long-term debt that the company has raised with the amount of capital provided by the shareholders. The ratio is calculated by dividing the long-term debt by the capital employed. (Remember that the capital employed is made up of the long-term debt, shareholders' equity and tax.)

ACTIVITY 32

A company that has a long-term debt of £1 500 000 and total capital employed of £300 000 would have a debt ratio of 50 per cent. If it increased its debt, would you expect this percentage to rise or fall?

FEEDBACK

The percentage would rise if the company increased its debt.

If the debt ratio rises too high, the company can be criticized for raising too much long-term debt. It could be said that the lenders are taking too much of the business risk, which should properly be borne by the shareholders. If the ratio falls too low, it could be said that the company is being too cautious and might be missing good profit-making opportunities.

The current ratio measures how easily the company could pay its short-term liabilities from its short-term assets. The ratio is calculated by dividing current assets by current liabilities. For example, a company that has current assets of £10 000 and current liabilities of £8000 would have a current ratio of 1.25.

The current ratio includes stock. It is sometimes felt that it would not be easy to sell stock quickly in order to meet short-term liabilities. The quick ratio, which is sometimes also called the acid test, disregards the stock and only considers other current assets.

ACTIVITY 33

Work out the quick ratio for a company that has current assets of £10 000, stock of £1000 and current liabilities of £8000.

FEEDBACK

This company has a quick ratio of 9 divided by 8, which equals 1.125.

If a company has a quick ratio that is greater than one, this gives us the information that it has enough assets to pay its short-term liabilities, if the need arose. However, this can be slightly misleading. Current assets include money owed by customers, which may or may not be paid when it is due.

INVESTMENT MEASURES

These measures assess how the company is performing from the point of view of an investor. One common investment measure is earning per share (EPS). This measures how much profit the company has produced for each ordinary share in issue. It is calculated by dividing profit after tax by the average number of ordinary shares in issue during the year. So, if a company had a profit after tax of £100 000 and 20 000 shares, the EPS would be £5 per share. A company would be unlikely to distribute all this money to its shareholders in dividends, but would retain some of its profit to reinvest in its activities.

Another common measure is the price/earnings ratio (sometimes abbreviated to the P/E ratio). This relates the earnings per share to the price currently quoted on the stock market. It can, therefore, only be calculated for public companies that have a stock market quotation. It is worked out by dividing the current market price per share by the earnings per share.

USING FINANCIAL RATIOS

We have only discussed some of the more common of the financial ratios that are used to assess a company's performance. A large range of ratios exist. It is important not to attach too much importance to one single ratio, but to use a number of ratios together in order to build up a more comprehensive picture of the company. If you went to the doctor complaining of a pain, you would expect the doctor to use a series of relevant tests to determine your physical condition. You need to follow a similar procedure to establish the financial condition of a company.

It is often helpful to compare the results of a company over a period of five years or more, in order to establish a trend. Many companies provide summary results for this period in their published accounts so that readers can make this analysis. It is also helpful to compare the ratios for one company with other companies in the same industry, although it is important to select companies that are as similar as possible to the company under review.

ACTIVITY 34

Conclude your work on this section by examining the annual accounts for the organization you work for. Work out as many of the ratios as you can from the accounts. Look for trends over the last few years. Present the results of your examination as a short report that you could use to explain the organization's financial situation and its future priorities to members of your own team who have little or no knowledge of financial management.

FEEDBACK

In the context of this book, it has only been possible to discuss the basic principles of company accounts. Hopefully, this will have enabled you to gain some insight into your own organization's financial statements. You will, however, probably have come across some unfamiliar terms and concepts in the course of this activity. If you feel you need to investigate the topic in more depth, we can recommend *Accounts Demystified: How to understand and use company accounts* by Anthony Rice, published by the Institute of Management Foundation and Pitman Publishing in 1993.

Summary

Now that you have finished this section you should be able to:

- explain the balance sheet equation
- distinguish between fixed and current assets
- draw up a simple balance sheet
- read a balance sheet with understanding
- draw up a simple profit and loss statement
- read a profit and loss statement with understanding
- draw up a simple cash flow statement
- read a cash flow statement with understanding
- calculate a selection of commonly used financial ratios from information on financial statements

Section 3 Looking into the Future

In Section 2 you looked at how organizations record and analyse their past financial transactions. In this section we turn our attention from the past to the future. We will explore some methods of forecasting which organizations can use when they are deciding how to spend their money.

You will need to use the techniques described in this section if you are making a financial case for a project. Like the previous section, this one also deals with subjects that are sometimes left to specialized financial managers. However, the principles involved are remarkably simple and you will probably find that you are able to implement the ideas and techniques you meet here in the context of your own organization.

The need to produce forecasts

There are two stages in the planning process at which you must consider the future financial implications of a plan or project. When you are putting a proposal to senior management, you need to give details of the financial costs to the organization and the benefits it will bring. Senior management require this information in order to decide whether they should invest in this particular plan, or in one of the others that are under consideration. As we described in the first section, effective planning involves having a range of options to choose from. The forecasts produced at this stage may look several years ahead, beyond the point at which it is possible to calculate accurate costings. However, their purpose is not to establish the exact details of any proposed expenditure, but to provide a clear basis of comparison between alternative options.

Later on, once a particular plan has been chosen, a forecast budget is worked out in more detail. This budget needs to be as accurate as possible. At this stage, forecasting techniques are used as a guide to the financial resources that will be required and to the amount of cash that the organization will have available for other activities.

There are three basic types of investment that a company can make in its activities:

- investments for growth
- investments which will reduce costs
- investments which will improve safety and maintenance

ACTIVITY 35

Can you think of examples of each of these types of investment from your own organization?

- investment for growth

- investment to reduce costs

- investment to improve safety and maintenance

FEEDBACK

Investments for growth often involve the development of a new product or movement into a new market. They may also be concerned with an increase in production.

Investments to reduce costs can involve the purchase of new plant or premises, or the adoption of new working processes.

Investment to improve safety and maintenance may involve the upgrading of premises or equipment or the adoption of new working practices.

The decision about which of these three types of investment a company is going to make will not be made on financial grounds alone. Other factors that could affect the decision include:

- new markets which are opening up
- changes in customers' requirements
- technological developments
- the economic environment
- what an organization's competitors are doing
- legal considerations, such as new safety legislation

- the underlying values of the organization

  In the example below, the values of the organization led it to choose to invest in maintenance rather than growth:

  Manager of computer games company
  Our first game was a fantastic commercial success. The company was awash with cash after the first six months, we could have done anything we wanted. One idea was to go for growth and get a lot of new games onto the market quickly. Anything with our logo on it would have sold immediately. But we realized that our success was due to the fact that we had an incredible team. We were small, but we were the best. We didn't want to become just another software company. The important thing was to keep that team together. So we spent a great deal of money in creating a superb working environment.

  In the following example, the activities of competitors led the organization to invest in growth:

  Manager of travel company
  For many years we organized package tours in the UK and Europe. There were other companies offering similar types of holiday and we saw that they were going for more exotic locations, such as New York or Australia. It was what the customers seemed to want, and we felt we had to follow suit and do the same.

The decision about what kind of direction an organization is going to take is taken at a strategic level. Financial considerations will have some impact at this point, but they are not the only factor to be considered. Once the overall strategy has been decided, the financial implications of the various options become more important.

Each type of investment has its own financial implications.

Investments for growth

If you are developing a new product, entering a new market or introducing a new process, you are likely to be taking the organization into unfamiliar territory. It can be extremely valuable to assemble a team with specialist knowledge of the new area.

ACTIVITY 36

Imagine that senior management have asked you to investigate the financial implications of manufacturing a new product for a market in which you have not been active before. You are arranging the first meeting of a team of consultants you have assembled to advise you. Think of six basic questions you would place on the agenda.

1
2
3
4
5
6

FEEDBACK

There are many more than six questions that you would need to ask, including:

- What is the size of the market and how is it likely to change in the future?
- What price would be acceptable to this market?
- What are the costs of advertising to this market?
- What are the costs of distributing to this market?
- What type and size of premises will we need, and how much will it cost?
- What machinery will we need, and what will it cost?
- What do raw materials cost and are these costs likely to change?
- How many staff will we need, and how much should we pay them?

Investments which will reduce costs

If you are considering putting money into plans in order to reduce costs, there may be other issues that need to be brought into the equation. For example, if you are looking at the costs of introducing a new training scheme, you should think about the effect of taking staff away from their normal work. If you are considering buying a new machine that will produce goods more quickly, it may also produce goods at a higher quality, which may increase sales. Some of these factors may not be immediately obvious to you and it may be worth discussing proposals with people who have different viewpoints.

Investments which will improve safety and maintenance

There may not be any choice about some improvements that are made to the workplace environment. There may be legal – and also ethical – reasons why a certain piece of equipment needs to be upgraded or fitted with a safety guard. If an organization is to stay in business in its present form, these improvements must be made.

Hotel group manager

New EU directives on the storage and preparation of food meant that we had to make major changes to the kitchens of one of our smaller hotels, or stop serving cooked meals. We looked at how much money was involved and could see no way in which we could recoup these costs. Regretfully, we shut the restaurant and replaced it with a coffee and breakfast bar, serving only snacks.

There may also be other improvements that are desirable, but not absolutely essential. Here, forecasting techniques can help you decide the best time at which to make these changes.

Forecasting techniques

We will now look at some of the forecasting techniques that you can use to evaluate financial investments. In practice, you may hand these calculations over to a colleague with specialist financial training or use one of the many software programs that are available to produce your forecasts. However, the basic maths involved is not difficult. It can be extremely useful to be able to do these forecasts yourself, or at the very least to understand the principles by which the figures have been produced.

PAY-BACK

This is the simplest method of forecasting which is used to compare investments. It involves calculating the period of time that a capital investment will take to pay for itself. For example, if a new piece of machinery costs £100 000 and will generate £20 000 cash for the business each year, it has a pay-back period of five years. Another machine, which would generate cash of £25 000 a year, would have a pay-back period of four years. An organization that was using the pay-back method to decide which machine it would buy would select the machine that had the shorter pay-back period. Some organizations set a limit of, for example, three years, in which an investment must pay for itself. The pay-back method is used to decide whether a proposal meets this criterion.

The pay-back method has the advantage of being easy to understand and quick to use. A great many organizations use it to make decisions about spending. However, the method has several serious shortcomings.

ACTIVITY 37

You are considering which of two machines your organization should purchase. Both machines cost £60 000. Machine A will produce £20 000 of cash inflow for four years and then be ready for the scrap heap, while machine B will produce £15 000 a year for eight years before it needs to be replaced.

Which machine would you buy if you were using the pay-back method?

machine A ❑ machine B ❑

Which of these machines do you think would actually be the better investment?

machine A ❑ machine B ❑

FEEDBACK

If you were using the pay-back method of evaluation, you would choose machine A, because this would pay for itself in three years (instead of four years, in the case of machine B). However, machine B would continue to provide income for much longer. This is a situation where relying on the pay-back method to evaluate investments would lead you to make the wrong decision, unless your priority was to increase cash flow in the short term only.

The most obvious problem with the pay-back method is that it does not measure returns over the whole life of the investment. Another disadvantage of this method is that it does not take account of when cash flow comes in, as long as it is within the pay-back period.

ACTIVITY 38

You are choosing between two projects, for which you expect the following flow of cash in and out of the business.

Year	Project A	Project B
0	–£10 000	–£10 000
1	£1000	£5000
2	£3000	£4000
3	£6000	£1000

Which project would the pay-back method of appraisal lead you to choose?

project A ❑ project B ❑

Which project do you think would actually be the better investment?

project A ❑ project B ❑

FEEDBACK

Here, both projects rate equally under the pay-back method of appraisal. After three years, both investments have paid for themselves. However, the cash will come into the business more quickly with project B and this is therefore the better investment.

£1000 that you have in your hand now is more valuable to you than £1000 in 12 months' time. This is because the £1000 that you have now can be invested so that it returns to you, with interest, after 12 months. Money has a time value, which any method of evaluating investments should take into account. Unfortunately, the pay-back method ignores the time value of money.

DISCOUNTED PAY-BACK

This variation on the pay-back method recognizes the time value of money. It is based on making an assumption about the interest which cash could earn over a period of time. If you think that you could invest your cash at an annual interest rate of 10 per cent, you can work out that £1000 that you have now can become £1100 in a year's time.

$$£1000 \times \frac{110}{100} = £1100$$

You can also work backwards and know that £1100 that you receive in a year's time is worth £1000 at present values.

$$£1100 \times \frac{100}{110} = £1000$$

You can multiply any figure that you will receive in a year's time by the same fraction and work out how much it is worth at present values. For example:

$$£1000 \times \frac{100}{110} = £909$$

This means that £1000 that you receive in a year's time is only worth £909 at present value, assuming an interest rate of 10 per cent.

If you are investing cash for two years, you must multiply by the same fraction again:

$$£1000 \times \frac{100}{110} \times \frac{100}{110} = £826$$

£1000 that you receive in two years' time is only equivalent to £826 that you have now.

These fractions are known as the present value factor. They are usually written in decimal form for convenience. You can find the figures for various discounts printed in discount tables. Many business software programs will also do these calculations for you.

Table 2 shows the cash flows from a project at a discount of ten per cent.

Table 2 Present value of cash flows at a ten per cent discount

Year	Cash flow	PV factor	Present value
0	–£20 000	1.000	–£20 000
1	£5000	0.909	£4545
2	£7000	0.826	£5782
3	£8000	0.751	£6008

Using the ordinary pay-back method, the project shown in Table 2 would appear to pay for itself in three years. However, if the cash inflows are seen at their present value, a different picture emerges. By adding up the figures in the final column of the table, you can see that the cash coming in from the project would only amount to £16 335 at present values.

The discounted pay-back method gives a much better indication of the value of an investment than the ordinary pay-back method. However, it still does not take into account the value of an investment after the cut-off point. This method is useful if you want to do a quick estimate of whether an investment is worth more detailed investigation.

ACCOUNTING RATE OF RETURN

This method is also widely used by companies. It involves taking the average profits of the investment and dividing them by the average book value. The average book value is obtained by taking the amount that the investment cost and deducting depreciation.

ACTIVITY 39

Table 3 shows how the accounting rate of return is calculated. Can you fill in the missing figures?

Table 3 Calculation of the accounting rate of return

Book value	**Year 0**	**Year 1**	**Year 2**	**Year 3**
Gross book value	£50 000	£50 000	£50 000	£50 000
Depreciation		£10 000	£10 000	£10 000
Accumulated depreciation		£10 000	£ **A**	£30 000
Net book value	£50 000	£40 000	£30 000	£ **B**

$$\text{Average book value} = \frac{£14\,000}{4} = £\,\mathbf{C}$$

Profits		**Year 1**	**Year 2**	**Year 3**
Revenue		£16 000	£30 000	£50 000
Costs		£4000	£5 000	£8000
Cash flow (revenue – costs)		£12 000	£25 000	£42 000
Depreciation		£10 000	£10 000	£10 000
Net profit		£2000	£15 000	£ **D**

$$\text{Average profit} = \frac{£\,\mathbf{E}}{3} = £\,\mathbf{F}$$

$$\text{Average accounting rate of return} = \frac{\text{Average profit}}{\text{Average book value}} = £\,\mathbf{G}\text{ per cent}$$

FEEDBACK

The missing figures are: A £20 000; B £20 000; C £35 000; D 32 000; E £49 000; F £16 333; G 46.7 per cent.

There are three main problems with the accounting rate of return as a method of evaluating investments. The first drawback is one which it shares with the pay-back method – it does not take into account the time value of money. In the example you worked through in the last activity, profits are not substantial until the third year of the investment's life. However, since they are averaged out over three years, this delay in receiving cash is not highlighted.

The second drawback derives from the fact that this method is based on figures for profit, not cash flow. As you are aware, these concepts are very different. By ignoring trade creditors and trade debtors in its calculations, the accounting rate of return can produce a misleading impression.

The third problem is less obvious. The accounting rate of return is a popular method of evaluating investments, but it is applied in slightly different ways by different companies. For example, some organizations work out the depreciation on assets differently in their accounts and this can distort the calculations. Some businesses will measure the capital invested in different ways, too. This makes it difficult to make comparisons between the accounting rate of return which various businesses achieve.

NET PRESENT VALUE

This method has many similarities with the discounted pay-back method.

ACTIVITY 40

Imagine that you have won a competition in a magazine. As your prize, you are offered the choice of £100 000 in cash or £10 000 a year for the next ten years. Which would you choose, and why?

FEEDBACK

You would be very foolish to choose the second option. If you invested your £100 000 in a building society, it would be worth substantially more than 10 x £10 000 at the end of ten years.

When an organization is considering an investment, it should think about the opportunity costs of the capital involved. These costs are equal to the market interest rate for investments of a similar risk. In other words, they are the amount that shareholders could get if they invested their money on the open market.

The net present value (NPV) method works by comparing cash outflow today with cash inflows in the future that are discounted at a rate equivalent to the opportunity costs. So, if shareholders could expect a ten per cent return on their money elsewhere, future inflows of cash would be discounted at ten per cent per annum.

The main difference between the net present value method and discounted pay-back is that NPV looks at cash inflows over the whole life of the investment, not just the time it will take to repay the initial capital invested. This gives a picture of the investment over a longer timespan and also takes into account the terminal value of the project, such as cash that can be realized by selling off machinery or buildings at the end.

Table 4 shows the investment you considered under the discounted pay-back method. This time, we have added two lines so that the table covers the whole life of the project. It shows that a cash flow of £6000 is expected in the fourth year and final year of the project. At the beginning of the fifth year, the plant purchased at the beginning of the project is sold off for £10 000, half its original purchase price.

Table 4 Present value for life of project

Year	Cash flow	PV factor	Present value
0	–£20 000	1.000	–£20 000
1	£5000	0.909	£4545
2	£7000	0.826	£5782
3	£8000	0.751	£6008
4	£6000	0.683	£4098
5	£10 000	0.621	£6210

If you total the figures in the last column, you can see that this project has a net present value of £6643. Because this is a positive figure, not a negative figure, this project will bring in a better rate of return than an investment on the open market. It is therefore an investment that the organization should strongly consider approving.

Net present value is an excellent method of evaluating investments. It is not significantly more complicated than discounted pay-back and it produces much more useful results.

INTERNAL RATE OF RETURN

Finally, we will consider one further method of evaluating investments. The internal rate of return (IRR) is based on the idea that an organization measures its internal investments against a predetermined rate of return which it expects the investments to achieve. The present cash outflows and the future cash inflows of a project are compared and a calculation is done to discover what the rate of return would have to be in order for these two figures to be equal. In other words, the rate of return is calculated for a situation where the net present value of the project would be zero.

There are several ways of finding the appropriate rate of return. Software programs often ask you to make a series of guesses until you reach the right figure. Once you have worked out the internal rate of return from a project, you can compare it with the predetermined rate that all internal projects must beat. If the project has a higher rate than this, it is worth investing in.

ACTIVITY 41

Project A will cost £20 000 and has an internal rate of return of 25 per cent. Project B will cost £50 000 and has an internal rate of return of 23 per cent. Using the IRR method, which would you choose to invest in?

project A ☐ project B ☐

Which project would bring in more cash to the organization?

project A ☐ project B ☐

FEEDBACK

Using the IRR method, you would choose project A, because it has the higher rate of return. However, project B would actually bring more cash into the business, albeit at a lower rate of return, and might in some circumstances be a more useful investment.

This activity drew attention to the main disadvantage of the IRR method. Because it gives you a figure in the form of a percentage, not an absolute amount, this can distort decision making in situations where you are comparing investments of different sizes.

ACTIVITY 42

Conclude your work in this section by finding out which method or methods your own organization uses to evaluate its internal investments. Does it use different methods for evaluating different types of investment? Are the methods it uses the most appropriate, in your opinion? Write some notes on what you discover.

FEEDBACK

This section has introduced you to the basic principles of several forms of evaluating the forecast financial returns from investments. In most circumstances, the NPV technique gives the best results, because it recognizes the time value of money and looks at the whole life of the investment. It also gives an absolute figure for the cash return to be expected, not a percentage rate.

Summary

Now that you have finished this section you should be able to:

- distinguish between investments for growth, to reduce costs and to improve safety and maintenance
- identify appropriate criteria for assessing these three types of investment
- describe the principles, advantages and disadvantages of several methods of evaluating financial investments

Section 4 Drawing up a Budget Forecast

Most organizations have their own procedures for drawing up budget forecasts. There are also many software packages available that can help you with your calculations and produce a professional document for presentation. If you work in a large organization, you will already have quite a lot of guidance available to help you with the mechanics of drawing up a budget forecast.

This section concentrates on the principles behind the process. It begins by asking you to think about the parameters within which your forecast is prepared. How does it relate to the wider strategy of your organization? Have any ceilings been set to spending or production – and are these limits immovable? You will explore how you can gather information you can trust on future expenditure and income and look at the various ways in which costs are classified. You will also be encouraged to look at your own budget forecasts with the kind of scrutiny that they will receive when you present them for approval.

Identifying the parameters

Your starting point when preparing a budget forecast is the strategy that your organization has adopted. This will tell you what you are trying to achieve. You may have been given precise targets for sales or expenditure – or you may have been given more freedom to interpret the organization's overall strategy at an operational level.

Our company is going through a period of retrenchment. I was asked to produce a budget forecast for my department which would produce savings of ten per cent in the next year.

Senior management were interested in developing information systems within the organization. They asked me to work out how much it would cost and the likely benefits in terms of increased efficiency.

LIMITING FACTORS

However much freedom you are given to interpret strategy, there will always be some limiting factors on your budget proposals. These could include:

- the amount of capital that the organization has available, or is willing, to invest
- the rate of return which the organization expects from its investments
- the size of the market you are serving
- the capacity of the plant and machinery
- the level of skill and training of the workforce
- the availability of raw materials
- contractual obligations
- legal obligations
- core services which you must maintain

ACTIVITY 43

Think about a budget forecast you have prepared, or helped to prepare, in the past. What were the limiting factors?

FEEDBACK

The limiting factors you identified may have originated either inside or outside the organization.

It is possible that some limiting factors are not quite as definite as they first appear. For example, a company may have a policy that all new investments in machinery must pay for themselves within two years. If you can show that a particular piece of equipment, while it will not meet this two-year rule, will produce substantial savings over a three-year period and continue to outperform its less expensive competitors, you may be able to argue for its purchase. (An understanding of the different methods of evaluating investments that you explored in the last section could be very helpful in this situation.)

There may also be other limiting factors that you can do something about:

Publishing manager

I had a fantastic proposal for a new series of atlases. There was a gap in the market which I was convinced we should go for. But the Board said that, although they liked my idea, we just didn't have the resources in-house. It would require some very advanced computer software, which we didn't have. And our editors just didn't have the specialized skills they'd need. So I suggested that we could put the project out to a production company. The Board was worried about the cash we'd have to pay out before we saw any returns, so I put forward the idea that we could reduce the initial outlay by paying the production company on a royalty basis. All we would have to come up with was an advance which would cover their expenses while the work was in progress.

ACTIVITY 44

Look back at the limiting factors you identified in Activity 43. Choose one that you would like to change. Can you suggest how this might be done?

FEEDBACK

Your answer to this activity may have involved a significant reappraisal of your organization's strategic or tactical plans. If you want to make a suggestion of this kind, you must be sensitive to your organization's planning process. If senior management has worked out their overall strategy some months ago, they may not welcome last-minute revisions. On the other hand, it may be possible to accommodate your suggestions within the existing strategy of the organization.

If your budget forecast is going to be controversial, it makes sense to explain your ideas to senior management at the earliest opportunity. Do not wait until you are presenting your completed budget forecast for approval. A meeting of a budget committee is not a good place to introduce senior managers to new concepts. Your proposals have a much better chance of being accepted if you have already persuaded key people to your way of thinking.

WHAT TYPE OF BUDGET FORECAST?

In the first section of this book, we mentioned some of the different types of budget forecast. Your forecast may include:

- costs
- expenses
- costs and expenses

You may be drawing up a budget forecast for all your department's activities, or just certain aspects of these activities, such as sales. You may be expected to include capital expenditure in your departmental budget, or to deal with this separately. If you are preparing a forecast for a one-off project, you may be expected to list start-up costs separately from running expenses. These decisions are likely to have been made for you.

ACTIVITY 45

Look at budget forecasts produced in your department. What do they cover? Give the titles and summarize the list of headings down the left-hand side.

FEEDBACK

Within an organization, budget forecasts are expected to follow a recognized format. This makes comparison and integration of different forecasts easier. You must be familiar with the conventions used within your organization.

INCREMENTAL AND ZERO-BASED BUDGETING

In some organizations, the process of preparing budget forecasts is simply a matter of updating last year's budget. In other organizations, the process starts again each time at square one.

Incremental budgeting is the traditional method of preparing a budget forecast. It involves taking the previous year's budget and adjusting it to meet the new situation. Adjustments could include:

- increases in prices
- increases in costs
- costs of additional activities
- reductions caused by deletions to the budgeted activity

The big advantage of the incremental approach is that budgets can be drawn up quickly, with little fuss and often with little discussion. The disadvantage is that activities are not reviewed rigorously, with questions asked about the relevance and usefulness of each activity. If activity levels have changed, there may be a much more efficient and cost-effective way of organising things.

In *zero-based budgeting*, all items in the budget need to be justified. The budget for each item is zero, until that item has been discussed and agreed by senior management within the organization. Items that have historically been included are omitted unless relevant or adequate justification is made for their inclusion.

ACTIVITY 46

What advantages and disadvantages can you think of for zero-based budgeting?

Advantages	**Disadvantages**

FEEDBACK

Zero-based budgeting encourages innovation. It can produce dramatic savings and efficiencies and helps to ensure that what is happening at operational level really does reflect the overall strategy of the organization. It also has several drawbacks. It is much more time-consuming than the incremental approach. It can lead to a sense of uncertainty among staff and to arguments among managers, all of whom are forced to defend their own corner. There is also a tendency for those managers who are the better communicators to secure more than their fair share of resources.

If your budget forecasting is done on an incremental system, it is still important to question what it contains.

ACTIVITY 47

B3.1

Choose an item of expenditure on a current budget.

Think about the alternative options.

Could the effect produced by this item be achieved in any other way? If so, how?

Would any of these alternatives be better?

If this item represents the best course of action, could it be funded in any other way? (And if so, how?)

Would any of these alternative methods of funding be better?

FEEDBACK

Your answer could help you to make changes like this to your budget forecast:

I thought about the amount we spend on publicity leaflets. Our response rate isn't particularly good, and I decided that it would be better to use some of this cash to purchase an up-to-date mailing list so that we could direct our mailshots more precisely.

Senior management spends an increasingly large amount each month entertaining clients in local restaurants. I realized that we could have a cook come in and prepare cordon bleu meals for less.

If we leased some of the equipment we need, instead of buying it outright, this would release capital for other areas of the project.

Gathering information

Once the framework for your budget forecast has been established, you need to gather information to put in it. This involves asking two essential questions:

- What is coming in?
- What is going out?

WHAT IS COMING IN?

If you are allocated money at the beginning of each year, this may be a very simple question to answer, although you may not know exactly how much you are going to receive at the time you are preparing your budget forecast. If you are generating your own funds through sales, the task of estimating how much is coming in is much more arduous.

There are three things you need to know about the money that is coming in:

- its type
- how much it will be
- when it will arrive

Type

The first distinction to make is the one between capital and revenue. Some of the money that comes in may be reserved for capital projects, such as the purchase of new equipment, while the rest can be used to finance day-to-day running costs. If your organization is financed either fully or partially from public funds, this distinction may be crucial:

Theatre manager
We got a grant from the lottery to renovate our auditorium, which was great. Unfortunately, the Arts Council cut our funding, so we could not afford to pay our actors. We were in the strange position of having state-of-the-art facilities which we could only afford to open to the public for three months out of twelve.

There may be other restrictions on how the money you receive can be spent. For example, certain funds may be set aside for training or for the completion of a particular project.

If you are generating your own revenue, it is important to classify where it is coming from. The way you do this will depend on what activities your organization is involved in and the information which it is useful for you to have. Here are some examples:

Garage manager

We classify our income as to whether it comes from the sale of new vehicles, the sale of second-hand vehicles taken in part-exchange, servicing, other repairs, petrol and diesel and revenue from the garage shop.

Sales manager

The sales forecast is divided into different products. I also have separate forecasts for each area representative.

Hotel manager

We have a computer program which analyses sales and provides us with a variety of different forecasts for the next budget period. I can get forecasts for the restaurant, rooms, the business suite and the bar. We have a certain number of contracts with large companies and I can get a forecast of what these contracts are likely to yield in the next twelve months, based on spending in the last twelve months.

Manager of industrial cleaning company

We have three large contracts with large organizations to provide a range of services on a regular basis. On top of this, we also provide extra cleaning services as and when they are needed. My budget forecasts for income are therefore divided into the contract payments, which I can predict exactly, and the additional payments, which I have to estimate.

ACTIVITY 48

How is the money coming into your own budget classified?

Do these classifications give you the information you need? If not, what other classifications would help?

FEEDBACK

Computer spreadsheets now make it possible to analyse historical data in a bewildering number of ways. You are only limited by the system of classification that was used when the data was originally entered. You have a similar range of options open to you in the headings you choose for your budget forecast.

When selecting headings for a budget forecast, there are two questions to keep in mind:

- Will this yield useful information?
- Can I check my forecast against actual figures?

Do not use a heading unless you can answer yes to both these questions.

Amount

If you are generating your own revenue, the amount you receive will be a function of price and volume. There are several factors to take into account when deciding prices:

- the price paid in the past for the same or similar goods and services
- what your competitors are charging
- the cost of producing the product or providing the service
- the level of profit your organization expects to make

Decisions about pricing are often taken at a high level within an organization and you may not have much input here. You are more likely, however, to be asked to estimate the volume of activity. In order to do this, you can analyse historical data and look for trends. You can also talk to people with specialist knowledge of the field.

ACTIVITY 49

A sales manager talked to three of her representatives about the sales that could be expected from a new product. Although all three had similar areas, they produced very different forecasts:

- 'I'll have no trouble at all with this product. I could probably move about 150 a week.'
- 'I would expect to be able to sell about 100 a week of these.'
- 'This one could be a bit tricky to place. Say about 50 a week?'

What reasons can you suggest for the difference in these forecasts?

FEEDBACK

Some people over-estimate what they can achieve because they want to impress you, or are frightened that you will react badly if they tell you their real projections. They may be deceiving themselves as well as you. Other people are over-cautious. They do not want to promise more than they are absolutely sure they can deliver. People may also deliberately give you a misleading forecast. If bonuses are paid after a certain level of activity has been reached, those concerned may want to keep that level as low as possible. Other people may not want you to know how much work they can get done in a certain time, because you will expect them to achieve the same level of productivity on a consistent basis. When you receive forecasts from individuals who will be responsible for achieving these targets, you may have to use your experience of what they have said in the past – and what they actually achieved – to help you interpret what you are told.

Timing

As well as estimating the amount of money that will be coming in during the budget period, you need to know when the cash will actually arrive. Many businesses fail not because of a shortage of orders but because of poor cash flow. Payment dates are likely to be some time after the date that products or services are provided, and many customers will not pay when they are supposed to. If you do not receive customers' payments yourself, it may be useful to liaise with your accounts department about payment records in the past. If you are dependent on a few large customers for your revenue, it could be worth asking members of staff who are in regular contact with these customers about how they appear to be doing. You may get advance warning about possible delays in payment.

WHAT IS GOING OUT?

Your budget forecast will also contain information about costs. You must obviously find out about the timing and the amount of these expenses – and also consider how you will classify them.

The range of cost headings usually include those related to:

- staffing, wages, pensions, training, etc.
- premises, rent, repairs, heating, etc.
- materials used, such as stationery, telephone, raw materials
- any other business costs, such as insurance

Descriptive headings such as these are easy to understand. There are, however, further ways in which costs must be classified.

Direct and indirect costs

Direct costs are those which can be associated directly with the production of a product or delivery of a service. They include the cost of raw materials, the wages of the people directly involved in manufacture and the cost of power and light necessary to make the product or provide the service.

Indirect costs are sometimes called overheads. They include the costs involved in distribution, administration, transport, advertising and anything else that the organization has to do in order to sell its products or services.

ACTIVITY 50

Look at this profit and loss account. It is one which you prepared earlier in this book.

Profit and loss account

		£
Sales		40 000
Cost of sales		
Raw materials	(10 000)	
Manufacturing expenses	(4000)	
		(14 000)
Gross profit		26 000
Operating expenses		
Administration	(2000)	
Advertising	(3000)	
		(5000)
Operating profit		21 000
Interest payable		(1000)
Profit before tax		20 000
Tax payable		(5000)
Profit after tax		15 000
Dividend payable		(500)
Retained profit		(14 500)

How does the concept of direct and indirect costs relate to the statements of gross profit and net profit?

FEEDBACK

To find the gross profit, you subtract the direct costs from revenue. To find the net profit, you subtract both direct and indirect costs.

Companies are obliged to state both their gross and net profit. The separation of direct and indirect costs is therefore essential. It is also extremely valuable for management to know how much of their costs are incurred in their core activities, which they are in business to provide, and how much in more peripheral activities.

Fixed and variable costs

Fixed costs are costs that remain the same, regardless of the level of activity within an organization. The rent that a company pays for its premises is an example of fixed cost – it does not go up or down, depending on how much business the company is doing.

Variable costs, on the other hand, go up or down depending on the level of activity. Raw materials used to make products are an example of a variable cost.

There are also some costs that are classified as semi-variable. These contain an element that is fixed and an element that varies. A telephone bill is a semi-fixed cost, because it is made up of a sum for line and equipment rental and a sum based on the number of calls made.

ACTIVITY 51

How would you classify these costs?

		Fixed	Variable	Semi-variable
1	stationery	❑	❑	❑
2	staff salaries	❑	❑	❑
3	wages of casual employees	❑	❑	❑
4	vehicle running costs	❑	❑	❑

FEEDBACK

I is a variable cost, because it depends on how much stationery is used. 2 is a fixed cost. 3 is a variable cost, because casual workers would only be employed when the level of activity justified it. 4 is a semi-variable cost, because it contains fixed elements such as insurance, road fund licences and regular servicing and variable elements such as petrol.

It is important not to confuse the distinction between direct and indirect costs with the distinction between fixed and variable costs. It is possible to have direct (or indirect) costs that are fixed or variable.

ACTIVITY 52

Think of an example from your own organization to go into each box.

	fixed	variable
direct		
indirect		

FEEDBACK

If you are clear about the difference between these two ways of classifying costs, this activity should have been easy.

Absorption and marginal costing

There are two ways in which organizations can apportion their costs.

With *absorption costing*, all production costs, whether they are direct or indirect, are treated as product costs and associated with the revenue derived from the sale of products or services. There is usually no problem about treating direct costs in this way. The organization must also devise a method of dividing up its indirect costs and spreading them out among its various products and services.

In effect, the process of absorption is a transfer of cost from some responsibility centres to others. To avoid disputes, this process of apportionment must be done on a basis which is fair – and seen to be fair within the organization. Common bases of apportionment include:

- number of employees – often used for personnel-related costs
- floor area – often used for rates, cleaning costs, lighting and heating and other building-related costs
- value of assets – often used for equipment insurance

When all indirect costs have been associated with a profit centre, they are then associated with the products and services that are provided by that profit centre by a process of absorption. Common bases for absorption are:

- number of units of output – used where the products or services are identical or similar to each other
- number of direct labour hours worked – used where the products or services are produced by a process that is largely dependent on human skills
- number of machine hours worked – used where the products or services are produced by a process which is machine-intensive

Most organizations estimate their costs, revenues and production volumes at the start of the year and then use this information to set their apportionment and absorption rates.

ACTIVITY 53

What would happen if an organization under-estimated its costs?

What would happen if an organization under-estimated its volume of production?

FEEDBACK

If an organization under-estimated its costs, it would pass an insufficient amount onto its profit centres and an insufficient amount would be absorbed by the price charged for products or services. The organization could find itself making reduced profits, or even a loss.

If an organization under-estimated its volume of production, too great an amount could be absorbed into the prices of the products and services. The organization might find itself making higher profits, or could find that its sales went down because it was charging higher prices than its competitors.

With a *marginal costing* system, only variable costs are treated as product costs and therefore associated with the revenue from products or services. Fixed costs, whether they are direct or indirect, remain with the cost centre that incurred them. Under this system, a product or service that produces revenue that exceeds its variable costs is said to produce a 'contribution' to the fixed costs of the organization.

Marginal costing has several advantages:

- it avoids the time and effort that would otherwise be spent on calculating absorption rates
- it avoids distortions caused by over and under-recovery of fixed costs

Under a system of absorption costing, as cost centres pass on their costs to profit centres, the need for careful control of costs may be reduced. With marginal costing, responsibility is clearly left with the cost centre that incurred them.

However, marginal costing is sometimes criticized for focusing managerial attention on revenue and variable costs (i.e. contribution) only. The fact that fixed costs also have to be recovered if the organization is to be profitable is sometimes not given sufficient attention. This may lead to a tendency to under-price the product.

Either system of costing can be employed in a budget forecast which is designed for use within the organization. However, for external reporting purposes, absorption costing must be used, because the cost of stocks must include all direct production costs, whether they are variable or fixed.

Many organizations now take another approach to costing altogether. Under an *activity based costing* system, efforts are made to apportion indirect costs on as accurate and realistic a basis as possible. This involves some research within the organization to find out what 'drives' the costs. For example, a computer manufacturer might look at the proportion of calls it received on its customer helpline in relation to each of its products. This proportion could then be reflected in the price of the products.

Drawing up the budget

When you have gathered your information, you can enter it into your budget forecast. Use a computer spreadsheet program to do this, unless your budget is extraordinarily simple. A spreadsheet will allow you to:

- check your figures
- update your figures
- present your forecast clearly and attractively
- explore the implications of any changes to the assumptions you have made in your forecast

Your budget forecast may take several forms, depending on what it covers. Conventionally, the various elements in the budget are printed down the left-hand side. The budget period is divided into separate periods, usually months or weeks, which each have a separate column. Each column is subdivided into three, with the estimated figures printed in the first subdivision. Actual figures are added to the second part of the column when they are available, and the variance between estimated and actual figures added to the final subdivision.

A framework is illustrated for a sales budget forecast form.

Framework for sales budget forecast

SALES BUDGET FORECAST 1997	Month:	Month		
		Est	Act	Var
Category	Volume			
	Price			
	Value			
Category	Volume			
	Price			
	Value			
Category	Volume			
	Price			
	Value			
Category	Volume			
	Price			
	Value			
Category	Volume			
	Price			
	Value			

A basic framework for a production budget forecast is also shown.

Framework for a production budget

PRODUCTION BUDGET FORECAST 1997	Month		
	Est	Act	Var
Materials			
Total materials			
Labour			
Total labour			
Overheads			
Total overheads			
Grand total			

ACTIVITY 54

Use Figure 3 to draw up a framework for the budget forecast used in your own department. (Do not put the figures in – concentrate on the headings.)

	Est	Act	Var

Figure 3 Framework for your own budget framework

FEEDBACK

The headings you chose will reflect the contents and purpose of your budget forecast, but your framework may take the basic form of one of the examples given above. Check that all your headings refer to things that can be monitored – and also that they will yield useful information. Did you remember to write in a title and a date and to specify the monitoring period? You might like to compare your framework with an example of a real budget forecast from your own organization. Check that you understand any differences between your framework and the real thing.

When you have drawn up your budget forecast, you may also need to prepare a separate cash flow forecast. This should contain the same headings as you used on your budget forecast, plus any other items that are relevant to the cash flow, such as loan repayments and the purchase of capital equipment.

Your budget forecast should include transactions at the time at which they take place and your cash flow statement should include them at the time at which payments are actually made.

ACTIVITY 55

1 You plan to purchase office equipment in mid-January from a supplier who demands payment within thirty days. In which month should you enter this item on:

- the budget forecast?
- the cash flow forecast?

2 You have a contract to do a certain numbers of hours consultancy work each month for a customer. You will be paid for this work on a quarterly basis, with the first cheque arriving in January. In which months should you enter this item on:

- the budget forecast?
- the cash flow forecast?

FEEDBACK

1 This item should be included in the budget forecast under January and in the cash flow forecast under February, when the cash will actually arrive.
2 One-twelfth of the total amount you will be paid for this work should be entered under each month of the budget forecast. The amount you will be paid each quarter should be entered under January, April, August and November.

Presenting your budget forecast

Before you present your budget forecast, you need to ask yourself some important questions:

- Am I clear about the organization's strategy and how it affects my area of responsibility?
- Is my information on income and outgoings accurate and up-to-date?
- Are there likely to be any changes to the income and outgoings?
- Are there any other factors on the horizon that might throw the forecast into chaos?

The last two questions are crucial. Step back from your budget forecast and think about all the things that could send it off course.

ACTIVITY 56

If the cost of labour rises or prices drop, your budget forecast could be wrong. Spend a few minutes thinking of any other factors that could affect it.

FEEDBACK

Compare your list with these points:

- sales rise or fall
- sales paid for later or earlier than you expect
- production costs rise or fall
- purchasing costs rise or fall
- administrative costs rise or fall
- personnel costs rise or fall
- any costs are paid later or earlier than you anticipate
- inflation rates change for the better or worse
- interest rates rise or fall
- taxation rates and thresholds change
- quotas change or are removed

If any of these changes are at all likely to happen, you must know the impact that this will have on your budget forecast. If you have assembled your budget forecast on a computer spreadsheet, these 'what if?' questions are relatively easy to answer.

SENSITIVITY ANALYSIS

If you are presenting the budget forecast for a major investment project, your 'what if?'questions may take the form of a sensitivity analysis. This involves looking at the major components of your budget forecast, such as:

- initial cash outlay
- volume of sales
- selling price
- production costs
- sales and marketing costs
- when income will come in

For each component, you must work out the percentage by which this figure would have to change to give you a negative net present value for the whole project. The components for which this percentage figure is lowest are those that are most sensitive to change, and therefore most critical to the success of the project. These components will receive the greatest scrutiny from the people who must approve your project. They are also the things that you must watch most carefully when the project is underway.

Submitting your budget forecast

Budget forecasts are often presented at a budget committee meeting. Prepare for this meeting as fully as you can. If the committee issues instructions on how budget forecasts should be drawn up, make sure you follow them precisely.

Find out who will be attending the budget committee meeting – and think about the kind of arguments that are likely to persuade them to approve your budget forecast. Read the agenda and consider the relevance of each item to your own forecast. Decide what you will say to introduce and explain your budget forecast.

ACTIVITY 57

Think about a budget you have implemented in the past that did not go according to plan. What questions should have been asked before it was approved?

Now try to anticipate as many difficult questions as you can about a budget forecast you are likely to have to present in the future. Could you answer them?

FEEDBACK

When you present a budget forecast for approval, you must be ready to answer questions such as the ones you have identified here. When you are introducing your budget, show that you are aware of potential difficulties, without, of course, going overboard and alarming the committee by describing how you would avoid problems that they haven't even thought of themselves. Have the figures ready, so that you are prepared to answer questions as they come up.

PREPARATION OF THE MASTER BUDGET

After the budget committee meeting, it is likely that some budget-holders will be asked to revise their forecasts. When this is done, the committee will draw together the budgets from all parts of the organization into a master budget. The first step in this process is often to prepare a profit budget and a cash budget.

The profit budget will probably look something like this:

PROFIT BUDGET	Month:		
1997			
	Est	Act	Var
Sales			
Less: direct cost			
Cost of materials			
Wages			
Gross profit			
Gross profit margin			
Overheads			
Salaries			
Rent, rates, water			
Insurance			
Repairs and renewals			
Electricity			
Postage			
Printing and stationery			
Transport			
Professional fees			
Interest charges			
Other			
Total overheads			
Trading profit			
Less depreciation			
Net profit before tax			

The cash budget may follow this pattern:

CASH BUDGET 1997	Month:		
	Est	Act	Var
RECEIPTS			
Cash sales			
Cash from debtors			
Capital introduced			
TOTAL RECEIPTS			
PAYMENTS			
Suppliers			
Salaries and wages			
Salaries			
Rent, rates, water			
Insurance			
Repairs and renewals			
Heat, light, power			
Postage			
Printing and stationery			
Transport			
Professional fees			
Capital payments			
Interest charges			
PAYMENTS			
VAT payable			
Total payments			
Net cash flow			
Opening bank balance			
Closing bank balance			

On the cash flow forecast, the difference between the opening and closing balance should be the same as the total of all the receipts and payments in each period. When a cash flow statement is produced, showing the actual figures, there may be some further reconciliation necessary to account for cheques and payments that the bank is in the process of dealing with.

Once the profit budget and cash flow forecast have been prepared, their contents are summarized into a:

- forecast profit and loss statement
- forecast cash flow statement
- forecast balance sheet

These documents, which form the master budget, are usually drawn up by staff with specialized accountancy training. These follow the same format as the financial statements you worked with in Section 2.

ACTIVITY 58

B3.2

Complete your work on this section by taking a close look at the budget forecasts produced by your own department. Also look at the guidance that is supplied to budget-holders to help them complete their forecasts. Check that you understand:

- all the headings
- any calculations which are necessary
- the procedures to follow to obtain and check information
- how budget-holders are expected to present their forecasts

Now write a short critique of the system used to produce budget forecasts in your department. Are there any ways in which it could be improved?

Summary

Now that you have completed this section you should be able to:

- identify limitations on a budget forecast
- explain the difference between zero-based and incremental budgeting
- gather information on income for a budget forecast
- gather information on expenditure for a budget forecast
- distinguish between direct and indirect costs
- distinguish between fixed, variable and semi-variable costs
- describe the advantages and disadvantages of marginal and absorption costing
- draw up a budget forecast
- prepare to present a budget forecast

Section 5 Keeping Control

Once your budget has been accepted, you must put it into practice. This final section deals with how you can monitor your costs and income during the budget period. You must have systems in place which give you ready access to the information you need to check your forecasts. But systems are not the answer to everything. The most stringent monitoring procedures in the world are useless if people do not apply them properly.

If you are going to keep control of finances, you need the co-operation and support of your staff. This section also explores ways in which you can encourage the people who work with you to help you stay within your budget.

Keeping track

All organizations have established procedures that set out who is authorized to approve expenditure of different kinds. These procedures are intended to make sure that financial resources are used for the purposes for which they were intended – and also are used in the most effective way. It is usually the budget-holder who has the responsibility for authorizing payments.

Quite frequently, the signing of an authorization is merely an official endorsement of a decision to spend money which has been made by someone else. If a signature becomes little more than a rubber stamp, this can have its dangers.

If a system of authorization is not enforced properly, there is an opportunity for fraud:

Office manager
We have a system for petty cash where I sign the receipt and recompense the person who has made the purchase. There was one young man in the office who, whenever he went out to the shop to buy some small item or other, never came back with a receipt. It was always 'Oh, sorry, they forgot to give me one' or 'I must have dropped it.' This was irritating, as I had to write out a special form instead, stating the amount, but he always seemed to remember exactly how much he had spent, so I didn't worry too much. One day, I happened to check the price of one item and discovered that he was overcharging us.

Even if no actual dishonesty is taking place, an ineffective system can lead to resources being wasted:

Manager in design consultancy

When we want to purchase something from a supplier, we write out a purchase order and the head of department signs it. She doesn't have time to check whether it's right or not. She just takes it on trust. Most of the time, this doesn't matter. However, I do know of some people who take advantage of the system. When they want to bring a freelancer in, they just ask him or her how much they think the job will cost and they write that amount on the purchase order. It's all too cosy and it makes a complete nonsense of the budget.

Some organizations introduce further controls on the authorization of spending, but fail to apply them properly:

Building maintenance manager

In our department, one manager puts in the requisition for the work and another manager checks that it is completed to standard. This is intended to be a safeguard against money being paid out for work that isn't done. If the same person ordered the work and authorized payment, it would be possible to set up an arrangement with a supplier where non-existent work was paid for. In reality, everyone in the office is rushed off their feet trying to keep up with their own work. There is no way that we can go and visit sites and sign off jobs which our colleagues have ordered. So what people tend to do when they need a job done is to get someone else in the office to sign the initial order. When the job is finished, they can then go and sign it off themselves. There's a nice, neat audit trail, with different signatures, and everyone is happy. However, the situation is wide open to abuse to anyone who wants to take advantage of it.

ACTIVITY 59

What could have been done to avoid the abuses of the system you have just read about?

1 Office

2 Design consultancy

3 Contract compliance

FEEDBACK

1 The head of department should question the individuals who raise purchase orders more rigorously about their contents and amount. It could also help to give these members of staff personal responsibility for parts of the budget. This might make them more frugal with the resources they are using.
2 The office manager should refuse to reimburse anyone who could not produce a receipt.
3 This situation is more difficult. The system needs to be changed so that no-one signs a requisition for work which they know nothing about. The head of department could make spot checks to ensure this is not happening and may have to reorganize the workload of staff to give them time to operate the system properly.

A system of authorizing payments that is unnecessarily complicated and time-consuming will encourage people to cut corners. This may lead to fraud. More often, it will lead to financial resources being wasted.

ACTIVITY 60

B3.2

Describe the system for authorizing payments in your department.

Are you aware of any ways in which people misuse the system?

How could this misuse be avoided?

FEEDBACK

As a budget-holder, you will probably be the last person to hear about the methods people use to get around the systems you set up. But you can use the experience you gained earlier in your career, before you were a manager, to do everything possible to ensure that your system of authorization is as watertight as it can be.

You also need to ensure that the money you **receive** matches the expectations set out in your budget. In particular, you need to know:

- if money is coming in on the agreed dates
- about changes to the prices you will charge
- about changes to the volume of orders which will affect revenue
- about changes to the nature of goods and services you supply which will affect revenue

Here are some typical problems:

Farm manager

We had an arrangement with a supermarket chain to supply speciality vegetables. We discussed prices and I put a figure in the budget which I was pretty confident we could achieve. However, six months into the arrangement, they suddenly told me that they were reducing the prices they were paying to growers. There was nothing I could do about it, because the contract was worded in their favour.

Marketing consultant

I did some training sessions for a company which I since discovered is experiencing severe cash flow problems. It's six months since I did the work, and I still haven't been paid.

Building contractor

I made the mistake of tendering for a job overseas without checking local building regulations fully. The work is taking fifty per cent longer to complete than I expected, with disastrous effects on my budget.

All organizations have systems to chase up outstanding invoices. It is often up to the individual manager to keep track of work in progress and check that it will in fact bring in the expected amount at the expected time.

Monitoring a budget

When payments or sales are made, information must be fed back to the budget-holder and compared against the budget. The system for monitoring a budget should follow three basic principles. It should be:

- easy
- regular
- completed at the lowest level

The easier a system is, the more likely people are to follow it properly. The system for recording financial transactions should be easy for the people who are inputting the information – and easy for those who are using it to compile data for budgetary purposes.

As far as is possible, use the categories of income and expenditure on your budget to code financial information as it comes in. If you can, avoid documents in which transactions of different kinds are mixed up.

When you prepared your budget, you will have broken down the budget period, which is usually a year, into shorter periods of a month or a week. These are the times at which you will have to make your regular reports on your budget. There is often a case for checking certain items more frequently.

ACTIVITY 61

Think about a budget you have monitored in the past. Were there any items on which you felt you had to keep a particularly close eye? Why was this?

FEEDBACK

The items you identified might have been:

- expenditure or income (or the timing of either of these things) which a sensitivity analysis has told you are crucial to the success of the project
- expenditure or income where you know there have been delays or difficulties in the past

The third principle for a system for monitoring transactions is that information should be recorded at the lowest possible level. This saves time and helps more junior members of staff understand the implications for the budget of their actions.

Most budgets are arranged in columns, with space to insert the actual figures against the estimated amounts.

SALES BUDGET 1997		Month:		
		Est	Act	Var
Category	Volume			
	Price			
	Value			

As well as gathering information about transactions that have taken place for the actual column, you also need to consider the estimated column. This involves:

- finding out about things that should have happened, but have not
- finding out about things that did not happen in the way you expected

When you fill in the actual column, you are compiling information from invoices, receipt books and other records of transactions. However, when you are examining the estimated column, your sources of information may be much less well defined. You obviously need to talk to people who are closely involved in day-to-day operations. You may also have to talk to customers and suppliers and to people outside the organization who have a broader view of the industry. These discussions will take time. They should not be completed at the last minute, just before you are about report on your budget, but should form part of your ongoing management role.

Getting the information

Budgetary information is passed to you from your team. You also need to pass information back to your team. The most important principle here is to recognize the difference between routine and non-routine information.

ROUTINE INFORMATION

You need to encourage your team to ensure that routine reporting is handled rapidly and efficiently. You can help them by making the system as easy to operate as possible.

ACTIVITY 62

Think about the system for recording and reporting routine transactions which operates in your department. Are there any points at which information gets held up?

Is there anything you could you do to improve the system?

FEEDBACK

Here is how one manager answered this activity:

When a purchase order is written out, it has to be coded. This involves looking the code up in a booklet. Lots of people don't bother and leave out the code, which means that the purchase order is returned to us by the accounts department. We could simplify things by writing all the codes on the purchase order. Then, all the person writing it out would have to do would be to circle the appropriate code.

Small, practical changes of this kind can increase efficiency tremendously. It may also be necessary to remind your staff about what they are supposed to do, and make sure that they are provided with clear instructions. There may be some sanctions you can apply to staff who do not complete routine paperwork efficiently.

NON-ROUTINE INFORMATION

There are some things that should not be left to the routine reporting system. You must establish a relationship with your staff which enables them to tell you about any activities which are not going to plan. It is essential for people to understand when a piece of information is important enough to bring to your attention immediately. This may involve telling your staff more about your concerns and priorities than you are used to doing.

Sales manager
I was desperate to receive a particular order from a customer. It had been promised for weeks and I really wanted to include it in the figures for the current month. It was only after I had submitted my budget report that I discovered that the order had actually arrived that morning, but nobody realized that I would be interested in seeing it quickly. It had been put with the orders to be included in next month's figures.

Do not expect your staff to read your mind. If you do not tell them when you need to know something, they may not guess. Even if you are very explicit about the things you want to be told about, you may still run into difficulties. There are many reasons why people are unwilling to give their boss unwelcome news about the budget:

- they don't enjoy being the bearer of bad tidings
- they have made a mistake and are afraid of the consequences
- they are protecting a colleague who has made a mistake
- they think they are going to be blamed for someone else's mistake
- they are deceiving themselves into thinking that the situation will just go away
- they hope nobody will notice
- they hope they can put things right before anybody finds out

You are most likely to be kept in the dark by members of staff who are more concerned with their own position in the organization than with your priorities as a manager. Encourage people to discuss their difficulties in a context where no blame is attached to them. Focus on how the task in hand can be achieved, not on mistakes which have been made in the past. Once people realize that you are more interested in resolving the problem than in blaming them for the part they played in creating it, they will be much more ready to be open with you in the future. Some managers are able to create an atmosphere in which everyone feels secure enough to discuss difficulties and setbacks openly. Other managers find that their staff are more willing to be honest in one-to-one discussions, rather than in front of their colleagues.

Read the following account of how a contract compliance officer working for a local council monitors his budget.

The Council has put the outside cleaning of its housing estates out to contract. I am in charge of checking their work at three estates in the Borough. The contract contains a list of scheduled work, which has to be done on a daily or weekly basis. I visit the estates every day and check that these tasks have in fact been completed to standard. If they haven't, I issue a default notice, and some part of the contract money is clawed back. On top of the scheduled work, there are additional tasks. These may be things I notice while I am going round, or things which tenants phone in about. I have an annual budget of £10 000 to cover additional tasks, which I divide into twelve equal parts in my budget forecast. I decide what is necessary to complete a task. It could be an hour of a labourer's time, or two hours with a mechanical cleaner, for example. For most of these things, there are set rates laid down in the contract and it's just a question of looking them up. If it's a major job, or something I'm not sure about, I'll call the Contract Manager at the firm of contractors and we'll have a site meeting and decide a price for the work. I have to be very careful not to overspend on my budget. Under the Local Government Act, I can actually be individually surcharged if I overspend. If I go a little way over one month, I may be able to pull back the next month. However, if I think my budget is not going to keep up with what I need to spend, I talk to my manager. He will either give me written permission to go ahead with a particular job, if I make out a good case for it, or he'll explain to his superior why the job is not going to be done.

ACTIVITY 63

What comments can you make on the way this officer monitors his budget?

FEEDBACK

The monitoring of the scheduled work appears to be handled well. Where additional tasks are concerned, the officer is encouraged to take responsibility for his budget by the threat of personal sanctions. He refers any decisions he is not sure about to his superior, who tells him what action to take. This officer is unlikely to overspend on his budget, but he may be afraid to take difficult decisions. His priority seems to be to protect his own back, rather than to solve problems.

REPORTING ON YOUR BUDGET

You also have to pass information up the organization about your budget. Routine reporting may be done on a budget control form, like this:

		Month			Year to date			Reasons for variance
Revenue		Est	Act	Var	Est	Act	Var	
Product	Volume							
	Price							
	Value							

Both positive and negative variances need to be explained, as both have implications for the overall finances of the organization. As a budget-holder, you may also be asked to provide a more detailed explanation of any variances.

This explanation should include:

- the reasons for the variance
- the implications
- any corrective action you are taking

The reasons for any variance can either be inside or outside your control. It is tempting to attribute as much as possible to circumstances which are beyond your control. However, remember that your managers are probably pretty astute and will have a fair idea of what really happened. If something does go wrong, you will actually make a better impression by admitting your failures, as long as you can show that you have learned from the experience and are taking appropriate corrective action.

You also need to think through the implications of any departure from your budget. Will other revenue be delayed or put at risk? Will costs (and therefore profits) be affected? Will the organization's overall cash flow be better or worse than expected? You do not have to spell out all these far-reaching consequences when you report on a budget variance, but be aware that these are the thoughts which will be going through the minds of senior management.

When you report a variance, you should also describe the corrective action which can be taken. In some situations, you may take this action on your own initiative, even before you give your report. If the problem is very serious, it may be better to go to a senior manager with a range of possible solutions and let him or her decide what to do.

Evaluation

At the end of a budget period, it is important to look back and evaluate the accuracy of your budget forecast and the effectiveness of your monitoring procedures. If you don't manage to stay within your budget, the questions in the next activity may be helpful.

ACTIVITY 64

B3.2

Answer these questions about a budget that you know about and which did not go completely to plan.

- What aspects of the forecast were wrong (timing, amounts of income and costs, volume of sales, nature of work, etc.)?
- Was this because circumstances changed?
- Could the changes have been predicted? If so, how?
- Was the forecast based on accurate assumptions?
- If not, how could information be improved?
- When did things start to go wrong with the budget?
- How quickly were the problems spotted?
- Could they have been picked up more quickly? If so, how?
- Was corrective action taken quickly enough?
- What could be done to prevent similar problems happening again?

FEEDBACK

The last question in this activity is the most important of all. Every budget you prepare should be an improvement on the one before.

Some managers are able to stick rigidly within their budgets. Their estimated and actual figures match each other exactly. If this applies to you, you may be extraordinarily talented in this area – or perhaps just extraordinarily lucky. There may, however, be some improvements you can make to your budgeting technique. Consider the questions in the following activity.

ACTIVITY 65

Think about a budget you know about which went exactly to plan.

- Were the targets for income or volume of sales high enough?
- Is there any way in which costs could have been reduced?
- Could the timescale have been reduced?
- Was the work covered by the budget completed to a necessary standard?
- Did anything else suffer in order that budget targets could be met? Was it worth it?

FEEDBACK

A budget that goes absolutely according to plan may be a genuine achievement. It may also mask other problems. For example, quality or staff morale may have been sacrificed, which could have long-term costs for the organization. It is also possible that the initial forecast was not ambitious enough. Many budget-holders also feel it necessary to spend up to the limit, even if this is not really necessary so that they are allowed similar costs in the future.

Even if your budget goes exactly according to plan, you may still be able to make improvements in the future.

ACTIVITY 66

B3.1, B3.2

Complete your work in this section by writing a set of recommendations to guide the individual who will be preparing and monitoring a budget next year. Base your recommendations on the budget you are working on at the present time. (This may be a budget that you prepared – or a budget that was drawn up by somebody else.) Use your experience of seeing this budget in action to make recommendations on improvements to:

- the way the budget forecast is drawn up
- the way the budget is monitored

Summary

Now that you have completed this section you should be able to:

- describe and evaluate procedures for authorizing payments
- design and administer systems for monitoring budgets that are easy, regular and completed at the lowest level possible
- encourage staff to keep you informed about anything which could affect your budget
- report on a budget
- evaluate how a budget is set and monitored

Summary

Now that you have finished this book, you should be able to:

- describe the stages in the planning process, from deciding objectives to making operational plans
- apply a model of the control process to your own activities
- recognize and overcome obstacles to effective monitoring
- draw up a simple balance sheet, profit and loss statement and cash flow statement
- read a balance sheet, profit and loss statement and cash flow statement with understanding
- calculate a variety of financial ratios
- distinguish between investments for growth, to reduce costs and to improve saftey and maintenance
- select and use an appropriate method of evaluating financial investments
- prepare a budget forecast, using zero-based and incremental budgeting
- gather information on income and expenditure for a budget forecast
- distinguish between direct and indirect costs and between fixed, variable and semi-variable costs
- describe and evaluate procedures for authorizing payments
- design and administer effective systems and relationships for monitoring a budget
- report on a budget